Nigel Cawthorne is the author of over 150 books – everything from *The Iron Cage: Are British Prisoners of War Still Alive in Siberia?* to *Sex Lives of the Popes*. His serious work has had him called to testify to the US Senate and questions asked in both houses of the British parliament. There are twelve books in his *Sex Lives* series – so he has done the dirty dozen. There are five in this *Old England* series and several other series are on the go. His book *Flight MH370: The Mystery* caused controversy worldwide. And there are, surely, many more to come...

CW01496565

Other books by Nigel Cawthorne

The Bamboo Cage – The True Story of American POWs in Vietnam
The Iron Cage – Are British POWs Still Alive in Siberia?
Daughter of Heaven – The True Story of the Only Woman to Become Emperor of China
Takin' Back My Name – The Confessions of Ike Turner
Reaping the Whirlwind – Voices of the Enemy from World War II
The Empress of South America – The Irish Courtesan Who Destroyed Paraguay and Became Its National Heroine
Sex Lives of the Popes
Sex Lives of the US Presidents
Sex Lives of the Great Dictators
Sex Lives of the Kings and Queens of England
Sex Lives of the Hollywood Goddesses
Sex Lives of the Hollywood Idols
Sex Lives of the Great Artists
Sex Lives of the Great Composers
Sex Lives of the Hollywood Goddesses 2
Sex Lives of the Famous Gays
Sex Lives of the Famous Lesbians
Sex Lives of the Roman Emperors
Strange Laws of Old England
Curious Cures of Old England
Amorous Antics of Old England
Sex Secrets of Old England
Beastly Battles of Old England
Flight MH370: The Mystery
Vietnam: A War Lost and Won
House of Horrors
Jack the Ripper's Secret Confession
A Brief History of Robin Hood
A Brief Guide to James Bond
A Brief History of Sherlock Holmes
A Brief Guide to Jeeves and Wooster
A Brief Guide to JRR Tolkien
A Brief Guide to Agatha Christie – Queen of Crime
The King of Crime Writers – The Biography of John Creasey
Outraged of Tunbridge Wells

Che Guevara

The Last

Conquistador

Nigel Cawthorne

Published as an ebook by Endeavour Press Ltd in 2014.

ISBN 978-1500166687 (paperback)
ASIN: B00I0BKFGK (ebook)

Website: www.nigel-cawthorne.com

Contents

Introduction

Like many other students in the 1960s, I thought that Che Guevara was a good guy—that he was an idealist who fought for the underdog, for freedom, justice, and liberty. But he was no working-class hero. He was a spoilt upper middle-class brat, a racist, a hard-line Stalinist, a Fascist sympathizer and a cold-blooded killer who was happy to put a bullet in the back of the head of his own men. No friend of the poor and disposed, he left a trail of misery and death wherever he went. Motivated by fanatical anti-Americanism, he was the Osama bin Laden of the 1960s. And he did not die at the hands of the CIA. Rather, after alienating all those who sought to befriend him, it was only the CIA that tried to rescue him. The revolutionary icon that adorns a million T-shirts is long overdue for re-evaluation.

Ernesto Raphael Guevara Lynch de la Serna was born the son of a wealthy architect and yacht-builder. In fact, he was a direct descendent of the last Spanish viceroy of Peru. Throughout his childhood, he was particularly close to his nanny. At school, he was fanatical about rugby and edited a magazine for rugby fans. He read the works of Marx, Engels, and Freud, whose books he found in his father's library at home. Although the young Guevara was impressed by the Republican refugees from the Spanish Civil War who fled to Argentina, he did not share his family's distrust of Argentina's Fascist leader Juan Perón. At Buenos Aires University, where he enrolled to study medicine in 1947, he compared Perón to Nehru, claiming that India's struggle for independence from Britain mirrored Argentina's struggle to escape the dominance of the United States. Later, in Cuba, he rolled the red carpet out for Perónists.

In 1949, Guevara made the first of his famous journeys, exploring northern Argentina by bicycle—later motorbike. These trips were sponsored by a Buenos Aires cycle shop. On his travels he met South American Indians and the rural poor for the first time. According to his own accounts, he found them dirty and smelly. He particularly criticized the Indians' insanitary and offensive toilet habits, though few places in South America had sewerage systems at the time. He was particularly critical of the personal hygiene of black people, who he distrusted and disliked. Being a pure-blooded Spaniard—though with a dash of Irish—he considered himself above other breeds, particularly gringos.

In 1951, he visited Chile, where he met Salvador Allende. He worked in a leprosarium in Peru and was arrested in Colombia during 'La Violencia,' though he had little to do with the fighting there. Later, however, he gave an inflated account of his contribution. This period of his life is covered in his memoirs by a chapter called 'The Proletarian Years.' However, his correspondence shows that he regularly wrote home, telling his parents not to send any more cheques and saying that he wouldn't be holidaying on the family's yacht that summer. This can hardly be considered proletarian.

Ending one trip in Venezuela, he managed to hitch a ride home—in typical Guevara style—on a plane belonging to a rich friend who was transporting polo ponies between Buenos Aires and Florida. However, on the way, the plane developed a mechanical problem and he was stuck in Miami for five weeks. Guevara described this stopover as the 'hardest and most bitter days of my life.' His friend said that they spent the time hanging out on the beach, drinking beer and eating French fries. How bad could that be? Guevara tried to make a little extra money cleaning the flat of a Cuban air hostess. But she found that he left her apartment in a worse state than he found it. He had never done any cleaning or tidying up before. His family had maids.

Back in Buenos Aires, Guevara went on to complete his medical studies in 1953, supporting himself financially during this time with various capitalist ventures, including selling second-hand shoes and a patent roach-powder he mixed himself, which he called 'Al Capone.' After deciding not to become a doctor, he headed to Bolivia where a revolution was underway. His travels led him to believe that Latin America was not a collection of separate nations but one single political entity—one that should be run by men of a nobler spirit like him.

He laid all Latin America's problems at the door of the US, which he hated. He ignored the fact that it was his Spanish forebears who had pillaged the continent, destroying the indigenous civilizations there. The worst were the settlers in Argentina who had made a concerted effort to exterminate the local Indian population. Hypocritically, in his writings, he made frequent jibes about the US policy toward the Native Americans in the Old West, which was positively benign by comparison.

Guevara was in Guatemala when the progressive regime of Jacobo Arbenz was brought down by a CIA-backed coup in 1954 and became convinced that the US would oppose any leftist government in Latin America. The only way to make his dream of a united South America come true was to kick the gringos out so that Spanish-speaking conquistadors, like himself, could take over. But the new rulers of Latin America would need anti-American allies. To that end, he became a hard-line Stalinist, supporting the Soviets even when they crushed the Hungarian Uprising in 1956.

It was in Guatemala that he acquired the nickname 'Che.' It was a pseudonym often given to Argentineans, who pepper their speech with the Italian interjection 'che.' Amusingly, it was pronounced with a hard 'c' like the gringo girl's name Kay.

After the fall of Arbenz, Guevara fled to Mexico where he met Fidel and Raúl Castro and other Cuban exiles who were preparing to overthrow the dictatorship of Fulgencio Batista in Havana. He was trained in guerrilla warfare by the Spanish Republican captain Alberto Bayo, who drew on his experiences in the Civil War. Meanwhile behind Castro's back, Guevara maintained contact with the Soviet embassy, putting the whole Cuban venture at risk. Thanks to Guevara, the would-be guerrillas were arrested, though Castro managed to get them released, persuading the authorities that they were nationalists intent on bringing democracy to Cuba, despite Guevara's hard-line Communist rhetoric.

Che was the only non-Cuban on Castro's 1956 expedition to Cuba on the motorboat *Granma*—purchased, incidentally, with CIA money. He was only allowed on the trip as the unit's doctor. But when the landing force was practically wiped out, Guevara became a *comandante* in the revolutionary army, fighting in the Sierra Maestra as Castro's right-hand man. Ruthless and aggressive, he was a disciplinarian who took it on himself to shoot his own men in the back of the head if they did not follow his diktat. When not fighting, he instructed his men in Marxist-

Leninist doctrine. Even Castro had to hide the fact that he was being funded by the CIA from Guevara as Che was an outspoken critic of anyone who did not follow a strict Soviet line.

When Batista fell, Guevara was hailed as a hero second only to Castro. He quickly gained a reputation for cold-blooded cruelty with the mass summary execution of Batista's supporters, as well as Castro's former allies who did not toe the Party line—even doing this Taliban-style in the football stadium. He killed so many people, without trial, that Castro had to beg him to stop. He opposed democratic elections, believing that only the Party could know what was good for the people. Directing agricultural reform, he expropriated the holdings of the large landowners, alienating the island's American investors and forcing Castro—who, until then, had sought to align himself with the US—into the Communist camp. A member of the reformist Ortodoxos party, Castro only became a Communist Party member in 1961. Meanwhile, as head of the National Bank, Guevara pushed non-Communists out of government and forced through disastrous Marxist reforms. Eventually, he had to go on Cuban TV and apologize in person for wrecking the economy.

Having abandoned his first wife and child in Mexico, he married for a second time in 1959, though he refused to take his new wife on a honeymoon when he traveled to Egypt, India, Japan, Indonesia, Pakistan, and Yugoslavia at government expense. Then in February 1960, as Minister for Industry, Guevara signed a trade pact with the Soviet Union who stepped in to bail out the basket-case economy Che had created.

Guevara had few friends in his new home. The Cubans distrusted him. As an Argentinean, he drank red wine and ate beef. Cubans ate pork and drank rum. They lived to party. He liked to stay home, reading and writing. He hated dancing; Cubans love it. Cubans also pride themselves in their many lovers. Guevara outwardly disapproved, though he cheated on both his wives. He set up Cuba's first Soviet-style labour camps on the remote Guanahacabibes Peninsula, the western-most tip of the island, and was not above sending adulterers there.

During the Cuban Missile Crisis in 1962, Guevara was, opportunely, *hors de combat*, having accidentally shot himself in the foot. He was furious when the Soviet Union pulled its missiles out of Cuba. He believed that they should have made a pre-emptive strike on major US cities. Knowing that the US retaliation this would have provoked would have wiped out Cuba, Guevara—an Argentinean—said that the Cuban people would be happy to die for the cause. No one asked them, of course.

In 1965, Guevara turned on his old ally, repudiating the Soviet Union for 'revisionism' and being a 'tacit accomplice of imperialism' by attempting co-existence with the US. He then flew to Beijing to seek an alliance with Mao Tse-tung who had fallen out with the Soviets in 1962. This prompted Moscow to threaten to pull out its support for the Cuban economy unless Castro got rid of Guevara, and so Che was forced out of government. He went to Africa to fight in the Congo alongside Laurent Kabila. Guevara's intervention was disastrous. He dismissed Kabila, though he eventually went on to overthrow the US-backed regime of President Mobutu. At the head of a force of 120 Cubans, he thought he could recreate the conditions in the Sierra Maestra and foment worldwide revolution. He neither understood nor trusted his African allies and had no interest in their plight. In return, they viewed him as a neo-colonialist, seeking to re-impose white rule on Africa. His intervention was catastrophic and the people of the region are suffering to this day because of it.

Guevara was eventually forced out of the Congo. No longer welcome in Africa or Cuba, he went to Bolivia in the autumn of 1966 to lead a hand-picked guerrilla band. The idea was to export revolution to the neighbouring countries from Latin America's most central state, so that he and his fellow Communist conquistadors could take over the continent. However, the Bolivian Communist Party, who were achieving power by constitutional means, did not want him there. The Communist Parties of the surrounding countries believed he was more trouble than he was worth, and he could expect no backing from Cuba, the Soviet Union or China.

Ill-prepared for the hardships of the jungle, his unit was almost wiped out on October 8, 1967 by a special unit of the Bolivian Army. Guevara was wounded and captured. No Communist country was prepared to intervene diplomatically on his behalf. The only people who tried to rescue him were the CIA. But the Bolivians felt that if they handed Guevara over to the Americans, it would look like they were in the pocket of the US. As they had no prison secure enough to hold him, the day after his capture, Guevara was summarily shot—suffering the same fate so many others had suffered at his hand.

Around that time a publisher from Milan had picked up a photograph of Guevara in Havana where there was no copyright to pay. When students took to the street in Paris in 1968, he printed copies to be used on placards and the picture instantly became the revolutionary pin-up for rebellious youth.

Both the picture of black-bereted Guevara looking off into the distance and the photograph of his dead body on a slab in Bolivia make him look Christ-like—though, with his fanatical anti-Americanism, he had more in common with that other rich-boy-turned-bad, Osama bin Laden. The parallels are striking. Both were spoilt kids from privileged backgrounds who wanted to change the world at the point of a gun. Both were fanatical ideologues who killed their own men with the same relish that they killed enemies. Both meddled in conflicts in countries that were not their own and volunteered to sacrifice other people's lives for the cause without consulting them. They were both motivated by a fanatical and unreasoning hatred of the United States, while knowing little about the country. And they both declared war on America.

However, Guevara, the conquistador bent on taking over Latin America, and then the world, found himself tilting at windmills and the giants knocked him down. Left-wing guerrillas in Latin America had been defeated long ago, or had entered the mainstream. After five decades of deprivation, Cuba is now embracing capitalism.

While Che Guevara remained a revolutionary icon on campuses in the West, little was heard of him in Cuba until 1991. But with the collapse of the Soviet Union, Castro sought to re-invoke the spirit of the Revolution. Guevara's image attracted tourists, whose foreign currency kept the Cuban economy afloat, while at home Castro's increasingly repressive regime used the image to hide behind. So it was a PR coup when Guevara's remains were unearthed near Vallegrande in Bolivia in 1997. They were returned, with due ceremony, to Cuba. There they were placed in a reliquary built on the outskirts of Santa Clara, where the last battle of the Cuban Revolution was won, and his canonization was complete. Throughout Latin America, the era of the *caudillo*, or strong man, is waning. These dictators were the men Guevara and Castro fought against, without ever recognizing the same traits in themselves. Democracy, American-style, is taking over and the people are prospering.

Guevara was undoubtedly a brave fighter. But his cause was hardly noble. Were the people of Cuba any better off under Castro than they were under Batista? Has insurgency in Africa improved the lot of those who live there? I think not.

The hard-line Communism that Guevara believed in failed because people did not want to live that way. They fled in droves whenever they had the opportunity. It is all too easy for disgruntled Hispanic intellectuals to blame all of Latin America's ills on its rich neighbour to the north. But it should be remembered that when the conquistadors arrived in South America they found lush, fertile land and wealthy cities, which they would ruthlessly pillage. The North was, by comparison, a barren plain with few resources. But what the settlers there brought with them was English Common Law, which allowed people to have title in their own property, and British electoral democracy, which allowed the government to change hands without bloodshed. This made the US the richest country in the world, while the wealth of the South was looted by those who pretended to be its liberators.

Nigel Cawthorne

Chapter One—Death of an Icon, October 9, 1967

Che Guevara was in a bad way when Felix Rodríguez first set eyes on him, lying wounded on the earth floor of the squalid mud-brick school house in La Higuera, a small village in the badlands of Bolivia. The legendary *comandante* of the Cuban Revolution was bedraggled and bleeding. He had been trussed up on the floor for nearly a day. His hair was matted and dirty; his clothes tattered and torn. He had no shoes. His feet were wrapped in crude sheaths of rotting leather, caked with mud. Fat and nearly forty, he was no longer the icon of youthful rebellion that he had been when he arrived on the international stage ten years before. No matter. The CIA had sent Rodríguez to rescue him. His orders were to keep Che alive at all costs.

'If he is captured, do everything possible to keep him alive—everything,' Rodríguez had been told in Washington.

Helicopters and planes were waiting to whisk Guevara to Panama and the safety of the Canal Zone, which was in American hands until 1979. Despite his pathological hatred of the Gringos, Guevara had been in back-channel talks with the Yankees for some time. At a conference instigating a US 'Latin-American Marshall Plan,' promising $20 billion to the countries of South America, at Punta del Este in Uruguay in 1961, Guevara had sought to open bilateral talks with the US, beginning the process by delivering two boxes of cigars to White House aide Richard Goodwin. One box was for him and one for President Kennedy, who displayed it openly in the Oval Office. Kennedy was an admirer of Che and after reading Guevara's revolutionary handbook, *Guerrilla Warfare*, that summer, gave the presidential seal of approval to the Green Berets.

Goodwin later met Guevara at a party in the home of a Brazilian diplomat in Montevideo. Kennedy was eager to learn who was getting more sex and Goodwin reported later in a secret memorandum that, when Guevara arrived, 'women threw themselves at him.' Then one of the Brazilians told Goodwin that Guevara had something important to say to him. They moved into an adjoining room and spoke for between twenty and forty minutes, though they were interrupted by waiters and autograph-seekers. Guevara was eager to continue, but Goodwin eventually broke off the conversation.

Communications didn't end with the death of President Kennedy. In 1964, President Johnson's National Security Advisor McGeorge Bundy had set up a meeting between Guevara and Democrat Senator Eugene McCarthy.

The American government knew that Guevara's life was now in danger. Castro had already torn up Guevara's Cuban passport, issued to the Argentinian after the Revolution. The Soviets wanted nothing to do with him because he had sided with China after the Sino-Soviet split. The Chinese wanted nothing to do with him because of his murderous incompetence in fomenting revolution in Africa. The Bolivian Communist Party wanted nothing to do with him because they had already obtained some measure of power through cooperation with the democratic government without any help from the self-proclaimed Stalinist. The Communist Parties of the surrounding South American states wanted no assistance from this bearded dilettante. That went for the Communist Party of his native Argentina as well, who knew that he had sided with the Fascist dictator Juan Perón and his homicidal wife Evita in the 1940s and 1950s.

*

Bolivia is a landlocked country that lies at the heart of South America. It is bordered by Brazil to the north and east, by Paraguay to the southeast, by Guevara's native Argentina to the south, by Chile to the southwest and west, and by Peru to the northwest. A Communist revolution there would create the perfect base to spread Communism throughout the whole of South America. This was Guevara's aim.

Most of the large cities are in the Andes Mountains to the west, which make up one third of the country. The lowlands to the east were sparsely populated.

Like most Latin American countries, Bolivia has had a checkered history. It was part of the Inca empire before the Spanish conquistadors arrived. Along with most of the Spanish colonies of South America, it became part of the Viceroyalty of Peru, ruled from Lima, and provided Spain with a wealth of silver. In 1776, it became part of the newly established Viceroyalty of Río de la Plata, run from Buenos Aires. Soon after, the Indians rebelled in the hope of re-establishing the Inca empire. The insurrection was put down with a huge loss of life.

At the time the country was known as Upper Peru, but when it gained its independence in 1825 it took the name Bolivia in honor of the liberator of much of Latin America, Simón Bolívar.

The War of the Pacific (1879–83) lost Bolivia its outlet to the Pacific and political power changed hands in a series of revolutions and coups. Border disputes continued, leading to the Chaco War (1932–35) against

Paraguary which left more than 100,000 men dead—making the Chaco War the bloodiest conflict in the Americas in the twentieth century. When both sides were exhausted, a peace conference in Buenos Aires gave Paraguay clear title to most of the disputed region, though Bolivia was given a corridor to the Paraguay river and to the port of Puerto Casado.

During the war, the military overthrew the civilian government and attempted to introduce socialism, seizing the assets of Standard Oil and installing a progressive labor code. When civilian rule was returned, the congress split between a pro-Soviet Marxist *Partido de la Izquierda Revolucionaria*, or PIR, and the initially fascist Nationalist Revolutionary Movement—*Movimiento Nacionalista Revolucionario*, or MNR. The MNR formed an alliance with a secret military group. Together they seized power in 1943, only to be overthrown in a bloody revolution three years later.

The PIR then tried to rule but was replaced with the more radical Bolivian Communist Party in 1950. The following year the MNR won the presidential election, but the military installed a junta. However, the MNR formed an alliance with a Trotskyite party that was supported by the mining union. In a series of revolts, the army was destroyed. The MNR took power, nationalised the three largest tin-mining companies, granted universal suffrage and instituted land reforms. Guevara was on hand in Bolivia to witness these reforms.

Many of the government's more radical socialist measures had to be reversed when inflation forced Bolivia to seek the financial support of the US. Standard Oil returned.

The military seized power again in 1964. However, General René Barrientos Ortuño (1919–69), despite being a vehement anti-Communist, spoke the native language of Quecha and, through the introduction of agricultural advances, managed to keep the support of the peasantry. This robbed Guevara of any indigenous support.

The Bolivian government also wanted him dead. They had been annoyed that the US government had opposed the summary execution of the French writer Régis Debray who had been with Guevara's tiny band of insurgents. There was no death penalty in Bolivia and no high security prison where a prisoner of Che's stature could be held. His trial would give him a damaging political platform and his imprisonment would make Bolivia the target for armed raids to free him or the blackmail of hostage takers. Nor could they hand him over to the Americans as this would make all Latin American anti-insurgency appear as if it were covert Yankee imperialism.

The Bolivian soldiers holding him were unsympathetic too. They were jubilant that the combat veteran of the Sierra Maestra and the Congo had been captured in little over a week by green troops who had not even completed their training. They had faced death at the hands of Guevara's foreign revolutionaries and saw no reason to extend mercy to their leader. The only people who wanted him alive, it seems, were the US government. But America could not be seen to intervene in the internal matters of a friendly nation, so they could not send a US national to get him out. They sent a Cuban instead.

Rodríguez could scarcely believe his luck. His immediate family had been on vacation in Mexico when Castro and Guevara had come to power in 1959 and they did not return to Cuba as the Revolutionary government had requisitioned their house and confiscated their property. He had watched helplessly from abroad while his extended family and friends suffered as the new regime's repressive grip tightened and the economy collapsed. Determined to do something for his country, Rodríguez joined the anti-Castro resistance, training in Guatemala and the US, and was later seconded into the CIA.

*

Born to a wealthy landowning family in Havana, Félix Rodríguez was seventeen when Fidel Castro and Che Guevara seized power in Cuba. He was already attending school in Pennsylvania. His father wanted him to go back to the US to complete his education, but Félix quit school to join the anti-Castro Cubans training in the Dominican Republic. At the time the dictator there, Rafael Trujillo, was fighting off a band of 250 Cuban guerrillas sent by Castro.

With the Anti-Communist Legion of the Caribbean, he set out to invade Cuba as Castro had done. However, the advance party was killed or captured. The invasion failed and Félix went to live with his parents in Miami. After graduating, he joined another anti-Castro outfit being trained by Frank Sturgis who had taught guerrilla warfare to Guevara in the Sierra Maestra and later found fame as one of the Watergate burglars. Then Rodríguez joined a bunch of Cuban exiles called Brigade 2506 who were training in Guatemala.

When Félix volunteered to kill Castro, he was flown to Miami where he was given a sniper's rifle. However, his three-man assassination team failed to get ashore and the rifle was taken away from him.

He was then sent into Cuba before the Bay of Pigs invasion. The infiltration was a disaster. He managed to escape arrest by taking refuge in a motel room with a hooker and was rescued in a fourth attempt to leave the island by a CIA boat. He returned with more guns and when the Bay of Pigs invasion was a failure he sought refuge in the Venezuelan embassy. After five months, he was given permission to leave. Returning to Miami, he went to work for the CIA full-time.

Known to the Bolivians as 'Captain Ramos', Rodríguez was at the headquarters of the Bolivian Army's Eighth Division in Vallegrande twenty miles from La Higuera when he heard that Guevara had been captured. He was installing ground-communication radios on their T-86 ground-attack aircraft when he heard the message: '*Papá* cansado'— 'Father is tired.'

'Papá' was the code name for a guerrilla leader and 'cansado' meant captured and wounded. *Papá* could either be the Bolivian leader Inti Peredo or Guevara himself. Rodríguez was eager to find out. He and the Eighth Division's head of operations, Major Serrate, climbed into the back seat of two T-86s. Serrate's took off first. Rodríguez followed. But minutes after leaving the runway, the cockpit filled with white smoke. There was an electrical fault. The pilot fiddled with some of the circuit breakers and the smoke dispersed, but in doing so he knocked out the mechanism that fired the plane's under-wing rockets and its .50-calibre machinegun.

But the radio Rodríguez had installed was still working, so they were able to talk to the Bolivian soldiers on the ground. Soon they heard that '*Papá—el* extranjero'—'Father is a foreigner.' It was Guevara. He had been wounded in his right calf and was carrying a large number of documents, including a diary.

Back at Vallegrande, Rodríguez reported to Colonel Joaquín Zenteno Anaya, who sent Lieutenant Colonel Andrés Selich of the Pando Regiment to seize the documents and interrogate Guevara. Rodríguez was worried. Selich was not a good interrogator. He had got very little out of a guerrilla named Paco they had captured earlier and had wanted to execute him out of hand.

'We've already told the press that the prisoner is badly wounded and is not expected to survive,' Selich said.

Rodríguez had stepped in and had obtained some useful intelligence from Paco, who had been tricked into fighting. The thirty-year-old upholsterer, whose real named was José Castillo Chávez, had considered himself a communist theoretician not a fighter. But he had been lured into joining Guevara's band with the promise of a revolutionary education in Havana and Moscow. Once out in the jungle, he had been given a gun and a *nom de guerre*. Selich had also been responsible for the 'disappearance' of Guevara's mistress, Haydée Tamara 'Tania' Bunke, who he had inherited from his bodyguard Ulíses Estrada, a black man whom he had fired. Guevara had little time for black people. In his eyes, like the South American Indians Guevara had such contempt for, they had little regard for hygiene.

'Blacks, those magnificent examples of the African race, have maintained their racial purity thanks to their scant affection for bathing,' he wrote in his *Motorcycle Diaries*.

During Che's African adventure, President Gamal Abdel Nasser of Egypt warned him not to play 'Tarzan, the white man among blacks, leading and protecting them'.

The Argentina-born Tania had also worked for the dreaded East German secret police, the Stasi. She had been with a group of guerrillas massacred at a river crossing. Selich took charge of the secret burial of the dead.

Even though Rodríguez did not trust Selich with his prize—Guevara—his assignment was a matter for the Bolivian Army, not the CIA, and he was in no position to question Zenteno's decision. Instead Rodríguez cracked open a bottle of Ballantine's Scotch whisky and toasted their good fortune with Zenteno and his divisional commanders. Afterwards, he asked Zenteno: '*Mi Coronel*, would you permit me to accompany you tomorrow morning to La Higuera to speak with the prisoner Ernesto Che Guevara?'

Naturally all of Zenteno's officers wanted to accompany him to see Guevara, but in the thin air of Bolivia the chopper could only carry the pilot and two passengers.

'I know that each of you wants to go with me,' said Zenteno. 'But Felix has been a great help to us, and I want to thank him for his assistance. I also know how important it is to him to come face to face with one of the communists who forced him out of his own country and how much it will mean to him to see Che Guevara. So if none of you have any objection, I will take Felix with me to La Higuera tomorrow.'

The following silence was broken by a voice saying: 'Yes, Felix must go.'

The other officers roared their approval. Zenteno raised his glass again.

'To Bolivia,' he said, 'and the return of peace to our country.'

That night Rodríguez prepared a long coded message which he sent to the US Embassy in La Paz. It told the CIA station chief there that, if the agency wanted to keep Guevara alive, they had better contact the Bolivian government quickly. The Army, he knew already, were not in the habit of keeping their prisoners alive.

At 7 am the next morning, Zenteno and Captain Ramos climbed aboard a small helicopter piloted by Bolivian Air Force Major Jaime Nino de Guzmán. It was a fine day and they made good time. At 7.30 they were descending into La Higuera, a tiny hamlet comprising a handful of mud-brick buildings along a single rutted track. They landed in a clearing near a small shack and a thicket of trees. As the rotor shut down, they could hear the thud of mortars and the rattle of small-arms fire from the surrounding jungle.

They were greeted by soldiers in combat fatigues. Selich was among them. He was not pleased to see the CIA man. They had had a falling out over the custody of the prisoner Paco and Selich did not want the prize catch—the *jefe guerillero* himself—taken away from him.

First Rodríguez and Zenteno examined the bag of documents Selich had seized from Guevara. It contained his diary and photographs along with the clandestine kit. There were one-time codes on tiny pads of rice paper—black for sending, red for receiving—microfilms and accommodation addresses in Uruguay, Mexico and Paris, which Guevara used to pass secret communications to Castro and other contacts.

Then they went to the schoolhouse where Guevara was being held. It was a two-roomed building in the centre of town with rough wooden doors and windows along the front. The tiled roof had disintegrated years before in the strong winds of the freezing Bolivian winter. Inside it was dim. Che lay bound on the earth floor. Beside him were the corpses of two Cuban comrades in arms whom he had led to their deaths. His arms were tied behind his back and his feet were tied together. In the next room was the Bolivian guerrilla Willy—Simón Cuba Savaria.

'Why did you come to Bolivia?' Zenteno asked Guevara.

There was no reply.

'How did you enter my country?'

Again there was silence.

'Why do you fight against my government?'

Standing behind Zenteno, all Rodríguez could hear was Guevara's breathing. The guerrilla did not even look up, and lay there with his head on the cold floor.

Guevara had not been so unforthcoming the day before when Selich has interrogated him. He had asked Guevara why he was so depressed.

'I have failed,' replied Che. 'It's all over, and that's why you see me in such a state.'

Selich also asked Che why he did not fight in his own country and why he and the Cubans had invaded Bolivia. Che insisted that socialism was the best form of government for Latin America and pointed to his two dead comrades, saying that although they had everything they could want in Cuba they had come to Bolivia to die like dogs.

'Are you Cuban or Argentine?' asked Selich.

'I am Cuban, Argentine, Bolivian, Peruvian, Ecuadorian... you understand,' said Guevara.

'What made you come and operate in our country?' asked Selich.

'Can't you see the state the peasants live in?' said Guevara. 'They are almost like savages, living in a state of poverty that depresses the heart. They had only room to cook and sleep in and no clothes to wear. They are abandoned like animals.'

'But the same thing happens in Cuba,' said Selich.

'That's not true,' Guevara shot back. 'I don't deny that in Cuba poverty still exists, but the peasants there have an illusion of progress, whereas the Bolivian lives without hope. Just as he is born, he dies, without ever seeing improvements in his human condition.'

Selich asked Guevara why he thought he had failed.

'I think it was lack of support from the peasants,' Selich suggested.

Guevara conceded that there was some truth in this, but also said that the country was too well organized politically and the army were well informed of the guerrillas' movements.

Selich then asked why Guevara had not managed to recruit more Bolivians to the cause, particularly the peasants of whom he talked. Guevara did not answer.

After a night in the schoolhouse Guevara had come up with no more answers to why Bolivia's political dissidents and peasants had not rallied to his cause. A sullen silence was the only reply he would muster to Zenteno's queries.

'The least you could do is answer my questions,' said Zenteno. 'After all, you are a foreigner and you have invaded my country.'

But Guevara said nothing. The only sound was the guerrilla's breathing and Zenteno indicated to Rodríguez that they should leave.

For Rodríguez, meeting Guevara had been an anticlimax. He had expected to be excited, moved or even shaken seeing his greatest enemy face to face. But he put his emotions aside. He had not come to Bolivia as a member of the Cuban resistance, but as an agent of the CIA—and there was work to be done. He got permission from Zenteno to photograph all the captured material. First Rodríguez sent off some coded messages, then laid Guevara's diary and other captured documents out on a table in the sunlight and photographed them with his tiny German Minox and a larger 35mm Pentax.

Zenteno had gone up to the forward command post and the Bolivians began bringing in more of Guevara's guerrillas. Juan Pablo 'Chino' Chang, a Peruvian of Chinese descent, and the Cuban Alberto 'Pacho' Fernández were already dead. Aniceto had been shot in the face. He was in pain and was held in the schoolhouse with Willy.

A telephone call came. Rodríguez answered it, identifying himself as Captain Ramos. The voice on the other end said: 'You are authorized by the High Command to carry out Operation Five Hundred and Six Hundred.'

Five hundred was the Bolivian code for Guevara. Six hundred was the code for execution. Seven hundred would have told Rodríguez that the Bolivian High Command wanted Guevara kept alive. Rodríguez asked for the message to be repeated. There was no doubt. The High Command wanted Guevara dead. He put the phone down.

When Zenteno returned, Rodríguez asked for permission to interrogate 'Señor Guevara' and, with Selich in tow, he went back to the schoolhouse. On the way they heard gunfire. Rodríguez rushed to the door of the schoolhouse and flung open the door. Guevara still lay on the floor and looked up at him. The shots had come from the next room.

Inside, Rodríguez found a soldier, the barrel of his gun still smoking. Willy lay dead.

'*Mi Capitán*,' said the soldier. 'He tried to escape.'

The windows were barred, the door guarded. Escape was impossible.

Rodríguez went back into the other room, where Guevara lay trussed. He looked, Rodríguez said, 'like a piece of trash.' As Rodríguez stood above Guevara examining him, he recalled how Guevara had once stood over his comrade Nestor Pino, one of the 2506 Brigade captured at the Bay of Pigs. Castro's men had already beaten him and left him to die, bound on an earth floor, when a pair of shiny boots appeared. It was Guevara. He looked down on Pino and said: 'We're going to kill you all.'

'Che Guevara, I want to talk to you,' said Rodríguez.

This time the *jefe* responded.

'No-one interrogates me,' he said imperiously.

'*Comandante*, I didn't come to interrogate you. I just came to talk,' said Rodríguez. 'Look at you. You used to be a minister of state in Cuba. Now you are like this because you believe in your ideals.'

Guevara agreed, if he was untied and allowed to sit up. Rodríguez called the guard to untie him. The man hesitated, as if he could not believe that such a dangerous animal should be unleashed. Rodríguez repeated the order and the guard complied. But Guevara had been tied up for a day and found it hard to move, so Rodríguez and the guard lifted him onto a wooden bench. Guevara then asked for tobacco for his pipe. Rodríguez had none, but got a cigarette from the guard and gave it to him. The guerrilla stripped the paper from it and tamped the tobacco into the bowl of his pipe. Once the tobacco was alight and he had taken several puffs on it, Guevara began to talk.

Rodríguez wanted to know why Guevara had come to Bolivia to start a revolution. Guevara said that he had considered other places—Nicaragua, Venezuela, the Dominican Republic, for example—but they were too close to the US. So he picked a country that was far enough away that a revolution there did not present an immediate threat. He also wanted a poor country and Bolivia was centrally placed in South America. It had borders with five countries so a revolution there could be exported to Peru, Chile, Argentina, Paraguay and Brazil. He had failed because the people there were too provincial.

'They wanted a Bolivian *comandante*, not a Cubano,' said Guevara, 'even though I am an expert in these matters… They cannot see their revolution in broad terms—as an international guerrilla movement working for the proletariat.'

But Rodríguez knew that Guevara was no proletarian. Like Castro, he was the son of a wealthy family. Castro's father was a landowner; Guevara's an architect and yacht-builder. They were two rich kids out to change the world at the point of a gun.

Then they talked about Cuba. Guevara admitted that it was an economic basket-case, though he blamed it on the US embargo.

'But you caused it,' said Rodríguez. 'You were a doctor, but you were made president of the National Bank. What does a medic know about economics?'

'I'll tell you a joke,' said Guevara, and he explained how he became president of the Cuban National Bank. 'We were in a meeting one day, and Fidel came in and he asked if anyone was a dedicated *economista*. I misheard him. I thought he had asked for a dedicated *comunista* and I put up my hand. So Fidel put me in charge of the Cuban economy.'

Guevara was reluctant to talk about his exploits in the Congo, but said that the Africans had let him down—'They were very, very bad soldiers.' He was also reticent about Castro, though he was plainly bitter that Fidel had not supported him in his Bolivian adventure. Without that support, Guevara had come to his present pass.

Nino de Guzmán wanted his picture taken with Che and they went outside. But Rodríguez deliberately altered the settings on the Bolivian's camera so that the picture would not come up. Guzmán then took a picture of Rodríguez and Guevara with Rodríguez's Pentax. The picture, the only one from that day, shows a youthful Rodríguez and tousled Guevara looking like a trapped animal.

Back inside, Guevara and Rodríguez resumed their conversion. It was then that Guevara realized that, for a Bolivian, Rodríguez knew rather a lot about him.

'You are not a Bolivian,' said Guevara. 'You could be a Cuban or a Puerto Rican. Whoever you are, from the questions you have asked, I'd say that you are working for US intelligence.'

Rodríguez confirmed that he was a Cuban.

'I was a member of the 2506 Brigade that operated inside Cuba, before the Bay of Pigs,' said Rodríguez.

Guevara's only comment was: 'Ha.'

The conversation came to an end with another shot from the next room and the sound of a body falling. Aniceto had been shot.

At 12.30 a radio message came from Colonel Zenteno from the High Command in La Paz. It repeated the order to execute Guevara.

Rodríguez tried to persuade him not to as keeping Guevara alive was of supreme importance to the Agency.

'Felix, don't ask me to do this,' said Zenteno, shaking his head.

Selich and the other officers wanted to keep Guevara alive too. They thought it would be better to show a defeated Guevara off to the world, then they could demand money from the Cuban government to give to the families of the Bolivian soldiers killed in the fighting. But Zenteno was adamant.

'If I don't obey my orders and execute Che, I will be disobeying my own president and will be given a dishonorable discharge,' he said.

Major Miguel Ayoroa, the commander of the unit that had captured Guevara, was put in charge of the execution.

Zenteno and Selich were heading back to Vallegrande. Zenteno would then send the helicopter back at 2 p.m. By then, Guevara was to be dead and Rodríguez was to return to Vallegrande with his body.

'The manner in which you deal with Che is up to you,' Zenteno told Rodríguez. 'You can even do it yourself. I know how much harm he has done your country.'

But Rodríguez had his orders and he knew how valuable the information Guevara carried in his head would be to the US government.

'Colonel,' he said. 'Please get them to try and change their minds.'

But if Zenteno could not get the order countermanded, Rodríguez promised to bring Guevara's body to Vallegrande.

Rodríguez still had hopes of saving Guevara's life. It would be easy enough. He could tell Major Ayoroa that he had received orders that Guevara was to be spared. When the helicopter returned, they could fly together to Vallegrande. There, once everyone had seen Guevara alive, it would be difficult to kill him.

But then Rodríguez thought back to what had happened with Castro in 1953 after he had been captured during an armed attack on the Moncada military barracks in Santiago de Cuba. The trial had given him a political forum and, even though he had been jailed, he had been released under a political amnesty two years later and had gone on to make himself dictator of Cuba. Might not Guevara do the same?

Besides, they were in Bolivia. It was up to the Bolivians to decide whether he lived or died. Rodríguez decided that he must leave the call to them. He was there to advise, not to command. It was appropriate that Guevara face a firing squad like so many of Rodríguez's friends had at La Cabaña Fortress in Havana, where Guevara had dispensed revolutionary justice.

'The executions by firing squads are not only a necessity for the people of Cuba,' Guevara said, 'but also an imposition by the people.'

Author Jam Philipp Reemstma compares him to Robespierre.

'There were over a thousand prisoners of war with more arriving all the time,' wrote a colleague. 'We did not even know all of their names, but we had a job to do. Che always had a clear idea about the need to cleanse the army and exact justice on those found to be war criminals.'

Nor were the new regime ashamed of what they were doing. High profile show trials had taken place in the sports stadium in Havana, in front of crowds of revolutionaries baying for blood. But, after Castro's visit to Washington in April 1959, three months after seizing power, he ordered that the executions were to be stopped. Guevara disagreed passionately. The enemies of the Revolution—and even some of its friends—had to be exterminated. Nevertheless, he obeyed.

And now it was Che's turn.

Rodríguez went back to photographing Guevara's documents when the village schoolteacher arrived.

'*Mi Capitán*, when are you going to shoot him?' she asked.

'Why are you asking?' Rodríguez replied.

'Because the radio is already reporting that he is dead from combat wounds,' she said.

That report sealed Guevara's fate, Rodríguez was now only postponing the inevitable. He went to see Guevara.

'*Comandante*,' he said. 'I have done everything in my power, but orders have come from the Bolivian High Command…'

Guevara knew this moment would come. In the Sierra Maestra he had killed enemy prisoners, just as he had killed his own men if they had not followed orders. When no one else had the courage to impose discipline, he had done it himself—even in training in Mexico—with the simple expedient of a bullet in the back of the head.

When Guevara heard that he was to face this same summary justice, he went white.

'It is better like this,' he said. 'I should never have been captured alive.'

Rodríguez asked Guevara whether he had any message for his family. Ever the revolutionary, he said: 'Tell Fidel that he will soon see a triumphant revolution in America. And tell my wife to remarry and to try to be happy.'

Rodríguez later said he stepped forward to embrace the doomed guerrilla.

'I no longer hated him,' said Rodríguez. 'His moment of truth had come, and he was conducting himself like a man. He was facing death with courage and grace.'

Outside the schoolroom, Rodríguez met Sergeant Mario Terán, who had volunteered to do the job. He had been in a firefight with Guevara's guerrillas the previous day and was keen to avenge three of his comrades who had been killed in battle.

'His face shone as if he had been drinking,' noted Rodríguez.

The cover story was that Guevara had died from wounds sustained in action, so Rodríguez told Terán not to shoot Guevara in the face, but from the neck down.

The death of Che Guevara is shrouded in myth. There are several versions of the story, but only two men were present—Guevara who did not live to tell the tale and Terán who spent the rest of his life in hiding. However, according to legend, when Terán entered the room, Che said: 'I know you've come to kill me. Shoot, coward, you are only going to kill a man.'

Terán fired a dozen bullets into Che's torso with a semiautomatic rifle. The first burst hit him in the arms and legs. Che bit his wrist to stop himself crying out. A second burst hit him in the chest, puncturing his lungs, which filled with blood. At 1.10pm on October 9, 1967, Che Guevara died.

Chapter Two—The Politics of the Pampas, 1928-1946

The legendary 1960s Cuban revolutionary Che Guevara was actually born Ernesto Raphael Guevara Lynch de la Serna in Rosario, Argentina—the third largest city in a country of 12.5 million people. His official date of birth is given as June 14, 1928, though it seems he might have been born a month earlier on May 14 as his under-aged mother was already pregnant when his parents eloped and married the previous November in Buenos Aires. His parents had mixed Irish, Spanish and Mexican blood. Grandparents on both sides had been born in the United States during the gold rush of 1848, but their families had returned to Argentina after the fall of the blood-thirsty dictator Juan Manuel de Rosas. Among his mother's family's more distant roots was General José de la Serna e Hinjosa (1770–1832), the last Spanish viceroy of Peru. He had taken over after staging a bloodless coup. He then lost 5,000 men in the fight against Simón Bolivar's independence movement. But then, until quite recently, most political activity in Latin American history was drenched in blood.

*

Occupying the southeast of the tip of South America, Argentina is about four times the size of Great Britain and a third of the size of the United States. The capital Buenos Aires was settled by the Spanish in 1536, but abandoned the following year. A colony was re-established there in 1580. Argentina was part of the Viceroyalty of Peru until 1776 when it became part of the newly created Viceroyalty of Rió de la Plata—also known as, the River Plate or River of Silver. Finding the grassy inland plains perfect grazing for cattle, the settlers set about exterminating the Indians who lived there. In 1816, the provinces of Rió de la Plata declared their independence from Spain. Bolivia, Paraguay, and Uruguay went their own separate ways. However, Argentina did not unite as a single country straight away. Instead each province was ruled by a regional strong man or *caudillo*. The most powerful was the blood-thirsty Juan Manuel de Rosas, who controlled Buenos Aires. He fell from power in 1852 and fled to England. A new constitution was adopted in 1853 uniting Argentina, but Buenos Aires refused to participate until it was defeated by the armies of the other provinces in 1860. Between 1880 and 1940, 3.5 million European immigrants arrived, largely from Spain and Italy. Meanwhile, democratically elected governments were frequently overturned by military coups. One such coup brought Fascist-sympathizer Juan Perón to power in the 1940s. Another in 1976 brought the junta to power, which invaded the Falkland Islands in 1982 and was responsible for the 'disappearance' of over 10,000 Argentinians.

Juan Manuel de Rosas was born to a wealthy family who owned some of the largest cattle ranches on the pampas. When he acquired land of his own he gathered an army of gauchos around him—the local cowboys—to protect his property from the Indians. In 1820, the governor of Buenos Aires, Colonel Manuel Dorrego, appointed Rosas head of the provincial militia. When Dorrego fell from power in 1828, Rosas, a federalist, opposed the new governor Juan Lavalle. He reconvened the former legislature which elected him governor in 1829.

At the end of his three-year term of office, Rosas stepped down. However his strong leadership made him very popular. In 1835, he was invited to become governor again. He agreed, but only if he was given dictatorial powers. For the next seventeen years, he ruled the country, using troops and his secret police to crush any opposition. Rosas even ordered that his portrait should be hung in churches and public places to show that he had absolute authority. In the end, armies from Brazil and Uruguay joined with Argentine dissidents under the command of Justo José de Urquiza (1801–70), the powerful governor of the neighboring province Entre Rios. They defeated Rosas at the Battle of Caseros in 1852. Rescued by the Royal Navy, Rosas was taken to England where he became a gentleman farmer in Hampshire. Meanwhile, Urquiza laid down the basis of a federal constitution uniting Argentina. It was adopted in 1853 but Buenos Aires refused to participate until it was defeated by the armies of the other provinces in 1860. Then in 1862, Argentina became a united country with Buenos Aires as its capital.

*

While Ernesto—soon nicknamed Teté—was born in Rosario, his parents' home was 600 miles up the Parana river in Misiones, on a plantation growing *yerba maté*—a local narcotic known as 'Paraguayan tea.' They were distinctly middle class. His father, also named Ernesto, had trained as an architect but, when his own father died when he was nineteen, invested his inheritance in a relative's yacht-building company in San Isidro, twelve miles along the coast from Buenos Aires. It was his mother Celia's money that had bought the plantation. She came from a radical family and grew up a socialist, anti-clerical feminist. She had been brought up largely by her older sister Carmen, a card-carrying communist who married communist poet, Cayetano Córdova Itúrburu, in 1928. Celia was her son's biggest intellectual influence until he met Fidel Castro in 1955.

Ernestito, little Ernesto, lived for the first year of his life on the plantation. He learnt to walk there, went riding on his father's horse and took excursions on the family's cabin cruiser up to the famous Iguaçu Falls on the Brazilian border. But there were dangers. His mother, who fearlessly went swimming in the coffee colored water of the Parana River, almost drowned when six months pregnant. The plantation was surrounded by jungle and Ernestito suffered from chiggers, a parasite whose larvae burrow into the skin. At night, his father would burn them off with the tip of a lighted cigarette.

In late 1929, the yacht-building company had gotten into difficulties and Ernestito's father left the plantation to take over. The family moved back to Buenos Aires with their nanny, a Galician who stayed with them for eight years. Soon after, the shipyard went up in flames. It was not insured, but the family was still well-off and they spent the summer on board their cabin cruiser, visiting the country estates of wealthy friends or swimming at the San Isidro Yacht Club.

On May 2, 1930, Celia took Ernestito swimming. It was already cold and windy, at the onset of the Argentine winter. That night, he had a coughing fit. This was diagnosed as an asthma attack. His aunt maintained that he had suffered pulmonary problems from birth and he may have inherited the condition from his mother. The remedies the doctor prescribed did no good and he suffered from the condition for the rest of his life. Whatever the cause, his father blamed Celia.

His mother and all the women in the family cosseted the sickly child. The asthma attacks continued. Even so, at the age of four Ernestito learnt to ride a bike. By June 1933, the attacks were occurring almost daily. No expensive was spared to alleviate his condition and the family moved to the spa town of Alta Gracia near Córodoba, whose fine dry climate attracted people suffering from tuberculosis and other respiratory conditions.

His father practiced as an architect there, while his mother brought up their growing family. Ernestito had two younger sisters, Celia and Ana María, and a younger brother called Roberto. Another brother, Juan Martín, would arrive in 1943.

During the next eleven years in Alta Gracia, Che's family moved regularly, moving from villa to villa as the lease ran out. However, his childhood was a model of stability compared to others at the time. In 1929, the Wall Street Crash had finished Ernesto's *mate* business and the collapse of world prices ended the dream of a free and prosperous Argentina. A coup followed in 1930. Meanwhile, peasants from the pampas fled to the cities to find work, further fuelling political extremism.

Perhaps because of his asthma, Celia and Ernestito developed a particularly close relationship. His illness kept him out of school until his was nine and he learnt to read and write sitting on his mother's lap. His father, resentful that his son's illness prevented him from returning to Buenos Aires, spent much of his time mixing with wealthy society in the Sierras Hotel, leaving Ernestito to be the dominant personality at home. However, it was from his father that he inherited his love of sport and the idea that willpower could overcome the limitations of his illness.

Che inherited a love of the countryside from both his parents and, as well as continuing his medication, he strengthened himself with swimming, riding and climbing hills in the nearby Sierra Chicas. He loved taking off into the wilds to escape the growing rows between his parents. By this time, his father's affairs with other women was a constant source of domestic strife.

Even so, his asthma confined him to bed for much of his childhood, which made him develop a love of reading. From his father he inherited an interest in the adventure stories of Robert Louis Stevenson, Jack London and Jules Verne. He also read Cervantes, Faulkner and Steinbeck. From his mother, he gained a passion for the French language and poetry. He read the original versions of Anatole France, Dumas, Zola, Verlaine, Mallarmé and Baudelaire. A fan of Frederico García Lorca, he also read works by many South American poets including Pablo Neruda and Horacio Quiroga. As adolescence dawned, he took to reading an unexpurgated edition of *A Thousand and One Nights*. And later came Freud, Marx and Engels, borrowed from his father's library—though, later in Cuba, he admitted that he had not understood a word of his early readings of Marx and Engels.

Eventually, the authorities caught up with him and, at the age of nine, he was sent to school. He did not excel academically, but he became famous among his peers for his daredevil antics. He drank ink from the bottle, climbed trees, explored an old mineshaft, hung by his hands from a railway bridge that spanned a gorge, and took part in 'bullfighting' with a notoriously bad tempered ram. With a gang of friends, he shot out the streetlights of Alta Gracia with a catapult and got even with a member of a rival gang by defecating on his parent's piano. He was regularly spanked—though, one day when he knew punishment was coming, he put a brick down his trousers and his teacher hurt her hand.

At school, he mixed with children from a broad range of social classes including other middle-class kids, the sons and daughters of the construction workers his father hired, the serving boys and the golf caddies from the hotels, and the dark-skinned peddlers who sold sweets on the streets of Alta Gracia. It was an open house at the Guevaras'. There were no fixed mealtimes, but Ernestito had to be careful about his diet. Some food—fish, for example—precipitated an attack.

Ernestito's father had been brought up as an atheist and, although Celia occasionally attended mass for show, she asked for her children to be excused religious instruction. She also had a reputation for being 'bohemian.' She was the first woman in Alta Gracia to drive a car, wear trousers or smoke in public. However, this was excused as eccentricity as she came from the upper classes. Her home became a salon for itinerate painters, poets, professors, and boot-blacks who stayed as long as they were hungry. It was a human zoo. To get some peace, Ernestito took to reading in the bathroom. This became a lifelong habit.

Like most young boys, Ernestito was interested in war and avidly read the press reports of the Chaco War (1932-1935) between Argentina's neighbor Paraguay and Bolivia. His father said he wanted to go and fight for Paraguay but did not go. This was followed by the Spanish Civil War (1936-1939). Guevara's uncle, the poet Cayetano Córdova Itúrburu, went to Spain as a war correspondent. Auntie Carmen and her children came to live with the Guevaras so they received regular dispatches from the front. Ernestito hung a map of Spain on his bedroom wall and followed the movements of the Republicans and Nationalists, and in the garden he built a miniature battlefield complete with trenches.

Soon Spanish refugees fleeing the fighting turned up in Argentina. Ernestito mixed with their children at his secondary school, twenty miles away in Córdoba, and became a fervent supporter of the Republican cause. He even named the family dog Negrina, after the Republican prime minister Juan Negrín.

His father helped found the local *Comité de Ayuda a la Republica* (Republican Aid Committee). Veterans were invited to the house for dinner to regale them with their war stories. These visitors included General Jurado, who had defeated Franco and his Italian allies at Guadaljara and was now selling life insurance, the composer Manuel de Falla and the Republic's former minister of health Juan González Aguilar, whose three sons traveled to school with Ernestito.

After the defeat of the Republicans, Guevara Lynch set up *Acción Argentina*, an antifascist organization that supported the Allied war effort during World War II. Ernestito joined the youth wing, attending meetings and undertaking investigations into infiltration of Alta Gracia's large German community with his father. Of particular interest to the Guevaras were the crew of the German pocket battleship *Graf Spee*, which had been scuttled off Montevideo after being cornered by the Royal Navy. They were supposed to have been interned in Argentina, but were seen undergoing military training.

The Spanish Civil War and World War II split Argentina politically between the nationalist, racist, Catholic, pro-Fascist right and the radical, socialist left. As a result, after World War II, Argentina saw the rise of Juan Péron, a Fascist sympathizer who, nevertheless, commanded the support of the masses and came to power.

*

A career soldier, Juan Perón was Argentina's military attaché to Mussolini's Italy in the 1930s. Returning to Argentina in 1941, he joined a plot which ousted the civilian government in 1943. He became secretary of labor and social welfare in the new military administration, giving him the opportunity to win the support of the *descamisados*—the 'shirtless ones'. He went on to become minister of war and vice-president. In October 1945, another coup sought to oust the military government and Perón was arrested. His beautiful mistress, the popular actress Eva Duarte, rallied the workers of Buenos Aires to force his release. A few days later, he married Eva—or Evita as she was known—and in February 1946 he was elected president. Politically, his regime was oppressive. Evita was said to keep a glass jar filled with the severed genitals of political opponents on her desk. Perón won a second election in 1951 with an increased majority, but Evita died of cancer the following year. A coup ousted him in 1955 and he went into exile in Spain. He returned in 1973 and was elected president once again. When he died the following year, his third wife took over. She was ousted in 1976. They left a continuing legacy of corruption and inflation.

*

While Perón had the support of the masses, he did not have the support of the Guevaras, who were anti-Perónist from the outset. Curiously, when in power in Cuba, Che maintained amicable relations with the Perónists, arranging a meeting between Perón and President Gamal Abdel Nasser of Egypt. Perón even wrote a letter to Che, congratulating him on the Cuban revolution, and Che even considered inviting him to come and live in Cuba.

Ernestito had enrolled in secondary school in Córdoba in 1942. The family moved there the following year. At school he excelled at sports and, at the Córdoba's Lawn Tennis Club, he swam and played tennis, golf and—in Anglophile Argentina—rugby. Small for his age until a growth spurt at sixteen, he played scrum half, a position that required leadership and tactical skills but not too much running. Vigorous exercise frequently triggered asthma attacks. He tried to overcome these with willpower, though he was sometimes driven from the field to use his inhaler or inject himself with adrenaline through his clothes. Nevertheless, on the field he was an aggressive player who earned the nickname '*El Furibundo*'—'the furious one.' He was also known as '*El Pelao*'—'Baldy'—because of his crew cut. He also became a proficient chess player.

Ernestito's father's business was doing well at the time but he squandered most of his money on his playboy lifestyle. He even brought home one of his lovers, the Cuban beauty Raquel Hevia, causing a scandal. The tensions at home took a dark turn and some people visiting the Guevaras' open house found themselves ruthlessly mocked by Celia and young Ernesto. The fabric of the house also suffered. Poorly built, Ernesto could see the stars at night through cracks in the walls. Although it was close to the Lawn Tennis Club, the house was surrounded by a shanty town. One of the favorite pastimes of the Guevara siblings and their friends was to watch the antics of the slum-dwellers. These included a dwarf who they bribed with sweets to show his curious white tongue, and a man with no legs who was pulled around in a cart by a team of six mongrels, which he whipped mercilessly. The slum children would throw stones at him. Ernesto begged them to stop, but this did not earn him the thanks of the legless man—only an icy stare. The conclusion Ernesto drew from this was that the legless man's hatred was directed towards not the poor children who tormented him but his class enemy, the rich kid who defended him.

Although he bought and read the works of all the winners of the Nobel Prize for Literature, Ernesto performed poorly at school. He was particularly bad at English. His daredevil ways continued, cycling along railway tracks and leaping from high cliffs into the river. He also loved shocking people. He earned himself other nicknames: *El Loco* and *Chancho*—'the Pig'—for his slovenly appearance and his boast that he seldom took a bath. But in 1945, a more serious side emerged. He wrote his own 165-page philosophical dictionary with quotations from Bernard Russell, H.G. Wells, Sigmund Freud, Friedrich Nietzsche, and, notably, Adolf Hitler's *Mein Kampf*. Other notebooks reveal that he was reading Lenin and Nehru, as well as Franz Kafka, Albert Camus, Jean-Paul Sartre, and Spanish translations of Walt Whitman and Robert Frost. He was also discovering Latin American literature.

Later his reading intensified. His brother Roberto was astonished to find that he had systematically read the entire twenty-five volumes of his father's *Contemporary History of the Modern World*. His notebooks reveal that he read everything from Aldous Huxley to the ancient Greeks via *Communism and Christianity* by R.P. Ducatillation, *The 1937 Socialist Yearbook*, *Das Kapital*, *The Manufacture and Use of Celluloid, Bakelite Etc.* by R. Bunke, *The Communist Manifesto*, and Alezandr Aleksei's *My Best Chess Games*. He also began to write poetry.

However, more than anything, he was fascinated by Marx. Later, while in hiding in Africa in 1965, he outlined a biography of Marx that he intended to write. Yet, as a young man in Argentina, it was Lenin that he modeled himself on.

These influences can be seen in the poems he began to write:

I know it! I know it!
If I get out of here the river will swallow me…
It is my destiny: Today I must die!
But no, willpower can overcome everything
There are obstacles, I admit it
I don't want to come out.
If I have to die, it will be in this cave.

Bullets, what can bullets do to me if
my destiny is to die by drowning. But I am
going to overcome destiny. Destiny can be
achieved by willpower.

Die, yes, but riddled with
bullets, destroyed by bayonets, if not, no. Drowned, no…
a memory more lasting than my name
Is to fight, to die fighting.

Around that time he also began to take an interest in girls. Unfortunately he was tone deaf and had no sense of rhythm so he was not much of a success on the dance floor. The tango was the only dance he could do. He had to be prodded in the back by a friend whenever one came on to remind him to ask a girl to dance. Even then, he had to count to keep pace with the rhythm.

He lost his virginity with his friend Carlos 'Calica' Ferrer's maid—'La Negra' Cabrera. His friends looked on through a keyhole and laughed when he stopped halfway through to reach for his inhaler. By seventeen, he was a handsome young man, with dark brown hair and intense brown eyes; girls found him very attractive. He took them to the pictures and read love poems with his beautiful cousin Carmen Córdova Iturburu de la Serna, known as 'La Negrita'. He also took up with the heiress María del Carmen Ferreyra, who he called *Chichina*, while at high school. They met at a wedding reception in Córdoba.

'I saw him in that house," said María. 'He was coming down the stairs and I was thunderstruck. He had an impact on me, a tremendous impact, this man was coming down the stairs and then we started talking and we spent the whole night talking about books.'

She dropped her aristocratic veneer and was 'completely enraptured.' The feeling was mutual. He wrote of 'those green eyes, whose paradoxical light announces to me the danger of losing myself in them.'

At the same time, he kept a secret back room in the Cecil Hotel, whether this was for his reading or to take other promiscuous *mucamas*—servant girls—it is not known.

When the military seized power in Buenos Aires in 1943, Ernesto's closest friend Alberto Granado was arrested for demonstrating against the coup. Ernesto visited him in jail and Granado asked him to organize another demonstration against his detention without trial. But Guevara was already showing his violent instincts.

'Demonstrate and get the shit beaten out of us with truncheons?' he said. 'I won't march unless I am carrying a gun.'

With his father away from home most of the time—taking off on his motorbike *La Pedorra*, ('The Farter,' so-called because of the spluttering that issued from its exhaust)—Ernesto took over as the man of the house, taking over the role of father to his youngest brother Juan Martín. And when he took his first job as trainee with the provincial highway department, he handed over some of his wages to his mother for housekeeping.

In 1946, soon after Juan Péron came to power, the Guevara family returned to Buenos Aires as Ernesto Senior's mother had fallen ill. They were in bad shape financially. Hearing that his grandmother was dying, Ernestito quit his job and hurried to her bedside to nurse her.

Around the time she died, his father and mother separated completely and Guevara enrolled in the Faculty of Medicine at the University of Buenos Aires, having decided to become a doctor rather than a civil engineer. This change in direction may have been caused by being there while his grandmother was dying. Another influence may have been that, around the same, his mother was diagnosed with breast cancer.

Guevara was serious about studying medicine. His apartment was soon filled with rabbits and guinea pigs, which he injected with carcinogenic agents. He also experimented on friends. And with a friend he cadged a foot from the anatomy theatre and carried it home on the underground, relishing in the other passengers' reactions.

Chapter Three – Latin American Journey, 1947-1952

While Guevara studied medicine in Buenos Aires, he followed his mother's treatment step-by-step with increasing anxiety. First she had a large tumor removed, then her entire breast was removed, along with her womb. At the same time, Guevara began to study his own condition, specializing in allergies. Later, he admitted to wanting to become a famous researcher. However, he was not a good student, attending irregularly.

Instead of studying he spent his time playing rugby and golf, reading philosophy and hitchhiking the 400 miles back to Córdoba to visit Chichina, who was now his fiancée. However, the political side of medical provision did interest him. He praised the National Health Service recently introduced by the Attlee government in Britain. However, he mainly stayed out of politics and, fortunately, the great guerrilla fighter was excused duty in the army—a Péronist stronghold—on account of his asthma.

To support himself, he founded and edited a short-lived rugby magazine called *Tackle*, bylining his own contributions 'Chango-Cho.' Then he came up with the idea of mixing a locust insecticide called Gamexane with talcum powder and marketing it as roach killer. He wanted to call it 'Al Capone,' then 'Attila' but eventually settled on '*Vendaval*'—Spanish for 'gale.' The young entrepreneur then obtained a patent and went into production. Soon the whole apartment smelt of Gamexane, but the project was abandoned when everyone got sick.

His next foray into capitalism was to buy up a job lot of shoes and sell them door to door. He ended up selling odd shoes to a one-legged man down the street. He wore odd pairs of different colors..

He did still take an interest in global politics and fell out with his father over the Korean War. His father supported the Americans, while Guevara was against them—though both shared a dislike of Coca-Cola. He pitted his Marxist view of history against his cousin's Catholic interpretation and appalled religious friends with his Nietzschean assaults.

While his parents were strongly anti-Péronist, Guevara himself was largely indifferent, perhaps because Péron's policies of nationalization and support for the poor robbed the Socialists and Communists of their base in the working class. Those around him in university were anti-Péronist, but as he supported the lower classes, his name never appeared among those of student activists.

In the face of his parents, he stuck up for Perón, writing to his mother after the fall of Perón: 'You must be glad… you'll be able to say whatever you please, with the absolute impunity granted you as a member of the ruling class.'

He even compared Péron to Nehru. His reasoning was that, while India was trying to establish its independence from Great Britain, Argentina was trying to escape the dominance of the United States.

According to Chichina's cousin and a friend of the young Ernesto, Dolores Moyano Martín, Guevara was fired up by an unthinking hatred of the United States from an early age.

'In his eyes, the twin evils in Latin America were the native oligarchies and the United States,' she said. 'The only things he liked about this country were its poets and novelists; I never heard him say one good thing about anything else. He would disconcert both nationalists and Communists by being anti-American without subscribing to either of their points of view. With much bad luck, since my mother was American, I would often rally to the defense of the United States. I was never able to convince him that United States foreign policy was, more often than not, the bumbling creature of ignorance and error rather than the well-designed strategy of a sinister cabal. He was convinced of the dark princes of evil who directed every United States' move abroad.'

Instead of involving himself in domestic politics, Guevara spent long periods alone in the library and having amorous adventures with numerous women, despite his engagement. He was seen everywhere with his fellow student and Young Communist, Tita Infante, and attended their meetings with her brother. However, he walked out on one occasion and was generally dismissed as a progressive liberal.

A relentless seducer of women, irrespective of their age or appearance, he was having sex with a Bolivian Indian woman in her late thirties, whom he called 'the ugliest woman I have ever seen.' He also had sex with the *mucama* of his strait-laced Aunt Beatriz and was once observed *in flagrante* with her on the kitchen table between courses at lunch.

'He was like a rooster,' said his cousin. 'He mated and then continued with his other functions.'

Meanwhile his long-distance relationship with Chichina, who was still back in Córdoba, intensified. Their physical attraction for one another was powerful, but otherwise they were ill-suited. She was from a wealthy family; his had fallen on hard times. She was elegant and well-dressed; he was slovenly, rarely bothering to press his clothes or comb his hair.

Dolores Moyano Martin recalled that while the other boys in their circle dressed well, Guevara developed his disheveled look for effect.

'Terribly clothes-conscious, all the boys we knew put a great deal of effort and money into obtaining the latest fads: cowboy boots, blue jeans, Italian shirts, British shirts… back then in the early fifties,' she said. 'Ernesto's favorite piece of clothing in those days was a nylon shirt, originally white but grey from use, which he constantly wore and called *La Semanera*, claiming he washed it once a week. His trousers would be wide floppy, and once, I recall, held up by a piece of clothesline. With Ernesto's appearance at a party, all conversation would cease, while everyone tried to look nonchalant and unimpressed. Ernesto, enjoying himself hugely and perfectly aware of the sensation he was creating, would be in complete command.'

While Chichina was light-minded, though cultivated, he was serious and intense. Her friends bored him, yet he had few of his own. Soon, she grew tired of the sullen adolescent.

'It was not out of malice, but there were things that irritated me,' said Chichina. 'I remember one time in Miramar, I was very irritated when we went to the casino. I don't know how they arranged it, but [Guevara's friend Alberto] Granado was very well dressed, and Ernesto was more or less dressed, I think. In the beginning it didn't bother me, but this time it did. A friend, or I myself, lent him a dress jacket, and then I think there was an admission fee, and he did something so as not to pay, to get the three of us in without paying, and that led to us being insulted. Then we went to various places where he didn't get along with people… Our group in Miramar was not very chic or sophisticated, they were normal, ordinary people from the Buenos Aires bourgeoisie, and he hated that kind of people.'

He then fell out with her father. During an argument over Winston Churchill—who Guevara described as another 'ratpack politician,' Don Horacio Ferreya lost his temper and leapt to his feet. Guevara remained seated. Grinning, he silently picked up a lemon and started eating it peel and all. This caused a rift with the family, but Chichina went on seeing him secretly. Eventually, the engagement was broken off because of his desire to travel.

Guevara had already traveled to the northern part of Argentina in early 1950, covering 2,500 miles and visiting twelve provinces on a motorized bicycle that he had built himself. The six-week trip was full of adventure, hampered by floods and volcanoes and complete with several brushes with death. He avoided the tourist destinations. Instead he visited hospitals, leper colonies, prisons and slept with tramps in an attempt to learn about the suffering of the people. Travel changed him.

'I realize now that something growing inside me for some time has flowered: it is a hatred of civilization, the absurd image of people moving like madmen to the rhythm of a tremendous noise that seems to me to be the hateful antithesis of peace,' he said. It was an adolescent gripe that he would not grow out of.

Even so, he was conscious of his image and he was not above hamming it up for the cameras. A photograph of him was used in an advertisement by the company that sold him the engine and sponsored the trip in return for an endorsement. It shows him wearing dark glasses, a cap, a leather bomber jacket and a spare tire draped across his chest like a bandolier.

He also cultivated the media. Along the way, he was interviewed by a local paper and was proud to see the first article about him printed. However, he began to see that the middle-class life he had led in Alta Gracia, Córdoba, and Buenos Aires with its yacht clubs, golf courses, and polo ponies was a luxurious façade under which the diseased soul of the country lay.

'I do not cultivate the same tastes as tourists... the Altar of the Fatherland, the cathedral... the gem of a pulpit and the miraculous Virgin... the Hall of the Revolution... This is no way to learn about a people, its manner of living or interpretation of life; that is a luxurious cover-up; its soul is reflected in the hospital bound sick, the prison inmates, the anxious pedestrian one talks with, watching the Rio Grande's turbulent flow at one's feet.'

In December 1950, he enrolled as a nurse on Argentina's merchant marine, traveling to Brazil, Venezuela, British Guiana, the West Indies and hoping to get to Europe. He was particularly taken with the Caribbean, writing paeans of praise for the passionate brown-skinned beauties of Trinidad. He had a fight with an American sailor in Brazil or, perhaps, an Englishman in Trinidad—accounts differ—confirming his animosity toward Anglo-Saxons. He also conducted an appendectomy at sea, using a kitchen knife. After returning to his studies, he headed off again on a motorbike with Alberto Granado who, a few years older than him, was now a doctor specializing in leprosy. He left Chichina with a mongrel pup which he named, in English, 'Comeback.' In exchange, in the back of her father's Buick, she gave him US$15 to buy her a headscarf when he reached the United States.

However, on the trip he wrote to Chichina, saying: 'I know how I love and how much I love you, but I cannot sacrifice my inner freedom for you; it means sacrificing myself, and I am the most important thing in the world, as I have already told you.'

Chichina had been expecting the brush-off. She had already decided not to wait for him and wrote to tell him so. He was devastated. Alberto wondered whether he was to blame for taking Guevara away, or for very publicly seducing the Ferreyra's *mucama*, in violation of the strict social convention that one did not sleep with the servant class.

On a Norton 500 christened *La Poderosa II*—'the Powerful One II'—they crossed the Andes into Chile, making repairs as they went. Perón later claimed that Guevara had left the country because the police were after him for avoiding military service. Perón himself had tipped the police off, not because Guevara was against them, but because of his anti-Perónist mother.

'Che was a revolutionary like us,' said Perón. 'The mother was the one who was not with us. The mother was the one responsible for everything that happened to the poor guy.'

Indeed, by that time, Perón was cracking down on the left. One of Guevara's friends from Córdoba, Fernando Barral, was arrested for 'Communist agitation' and held for seven months. The son of a famous sculptor, a Spanish Republican killed in the defense of Madrid, Barral was to be deported back to Franco's Spain to an uncertain fate, but at the last moment Hungary offered to take him as a political exile.

Eventually Guevara and Granado had to abandon the motorbike in Santiago. Along the way they slept in prison cells and barns, scrounged food and drink and attracted a good deal of press attention. They got into numerous scrapes and were chased out of town on at least three occasions after Guevara tried drunkenly to seduce a married woman, shot their host's Alsatian, mistaking it for a puma, and vomited on peaches left out to dry in the sun.

From Santiago, they headed for Valparasío, intent on traveling to Rapa Nui near Easter Island. They had volunteered to work on a leper colony there. Despite the horrendous deformities caused by their condition, Guevara had a particular interest in lepers and lectured others 'on the importance for the lepers' psyches of the friendly way in which we treated them.' However, it is clear that, in this case, he was more interested in the compliant native beauties of Rapa Nui he had heard so much about. He wrote of the delights he hoped to find: 'There, to have a white boyfriend is an honor for the females. There—what a wish—women do all the work. One eats, sleeps and keeps them content … What would it matter to stay a year there, who cares about work, studies, family, etc.'

However, the ship to Easter Island did not sail for six months. Supporting themselves by the generosity of others, Guevara earned a few centavos practicing as a doctor to the poor, though he had yet to qualify. Then they resumed their original itinerary.

They stowed away on a ship that took them to Antofagasta in northern Chile. There, they tried to stow away again, but this time they were caught before the ship sailed. There was a stack of melons under the tarpaulin where they hid. The ravenous pair had been eating them and throwing the skins overboard, which had alerted the captain.

From Antofagasta, they tried hitchhiking inland as they were intent on visiting the Chuquicamata copper mine. As the world's largest open-cast mine, producing 20 per cent of the world's copper, it was the principal source of Chile's wealth. And it was owned by Americans, specifically the family of Spruille Braden who, as US assistant secretary of state, had been accused of interfering with the elections in Argentina. At the time, the Chileans were discontent with the share of revenue they were receiving on a fluctuating market and there were calls to nationalize the mine. The US responded by putting pressure on the Chilean government to outlaw the Communist party and break up the mining unions.

Stuck in the middle of the Atacama Desert at night on the way, they met a marooned couple. The man had just been released from jail after being arrested for striking. Others had disappeared after their arrest and he feared they had been murdered. Guevara wrote: 'The couple, numb with cold, snuggling together, were a living representation of the proletariat the world over. They did not even have a miserable blanket to cover themselves, so we gave them one of ours. With the other Alberto and I covered ourselves as best we could. It was one of the coldest nights I have ever spent, but it was also one which made me feel closest to this strange, to me anyway, human species.'

In the morning, they got a lift to the mine. There Guevara saw 'the blond and efficient, insolent administrators… the Yankee masters.' He was given a tour by a Chilean whom he dismissed as 'the faithful dog of the Yankee masters.' But even he was dismissive of his bosses. A strike was brewing, he said: 'Imbecile gringos, they lose millions of pesos a day in a strike in order to deny a few centavos more to a poor worker.'

Guevara's biographer Jean Cormier identifies this as a key moment in the formation of the revolutionary Ernesto was about to become.

'It was at Chuquicamata between March 13 and 16, 1952, that Ernesto Guevara starts to become Che,' writes Cormier. 'After Chuquicamata, he is in a state of revolutionary incubation.'

Guevara was appalled by the sanitary conditions in Chile which, unlike Argentina, did not have any sewage plants. The Indians squatted wherever they chose, with the women wiping themselves and their children with their petticoats. But Guevara saw a solution to Chile's problems. With its abundant mineral resources, he wrote, 'the main thing Chile has to do is get its tiresome Yankee friend off its back, a Herculean task, at least for the moment, given the huge US investment and the ease with which it can bring economic pressure to beat whenever their interests are threatened.'

'An economic and political battle is being waged in Chile between the leftists and nationalists who support nationalizing the mines and those who, in the name of free enterprise, think it better to have a well-run mine (even if it is in foreign hands), rather than one subject to dubious management of the state… Whatever the outcome of the battle, it would be as well not to forget the lesson taught by the miners' cemeteries, which contain only a few of the enormous number of people devoured by cave-ins, silicosis and the infernal mountain climate.'

There was, however, a chink of light. While Guevara was in Chile, there was a presidential election. He was impressed by the Marxist Salvador Allende, who was standing for the first time. But Allende came last in a field of four as Communist voters had been excluded from the polls. The winner was General Carlos Ibañez del Campo, a former right-wing dictator who had now adopted a Perónist line and included the nationalization of the mines in his manifesto. However, his anti-Americanism precipitated a balance-of-payments crisis. The IMF stepped in and mine nationalization was dropped. Allende, however, was elected president in 1970, though he died in a military coup backed by the CIA two years later.

Next Guevara and Granado headed for Peru, visiting Lake Titicaca, 12,500 feet above sea level. In Peru, Guevara became very conscious of what he called the 'beaten race'—the native people. In Argentina, they had been practically wiped out and replaced by massive immigration from Europe. But in Peru the indigenous people were present and clearly subjugated.

While the Indians they saw lived in appalling conditions, the two travelers—being white, professional, upper-middle class, and Argentine—were afforded lavish hospitality. The local *Guardia Civil* put them up, in one case even paying for a hotel. As they hitchhiked around in their filthy, lice-ridden ponchos, they were asked about the 'marvelous land of Perón, where the poor have the same rights as the rich.' They did not have the heart to tell them the truth.

They visited the ruins of the Inca capital, Cuzco, and stayed for free in a tourist inn at the ancient fortress city of Machu Picchu, only to be kicked out after two days to make room for American tourists.

Speaking of Machu Picchu, Guevara said: 'We find ourselves here before a pure expression of the most powerful indigenous civilization of America, untouched by any contact with the victorious armies and full of evocative treasures amidst its dead walls, or in the marvelous landscape surrounding it and giving it a frame that will drive any dreamer to ecstasy.'

In his *Motorcycle Diaries*, Guevara rails against American tourists who traveled to the ruins in comfortable buses without ever giving a thought to the conditions of the local people. Although Guevara was descended from the Spaniards who had brought death and injustice to the native peoples, he felt that they were bound together by a common language and common problems. In a speech given on his birthday, drunk on the local *pisco*, a type of gin, he claimed that the division of Latin America into separate and unstable nations was a fiction.

'We are one single *mestizo* race,' he said, 'from Mexico down to the Megellan Straits.'

He called for Latinos to break free from parochialism and proposed a toast to 'Peru and a United America.'

The common enemy were the Anglo-Saxons to the north. The cold war was at its height and the US supported a raft of vicious dictators in Latin America—Anastasio Somoza in Nicaragua, Rafael Trujillo in the Dominican Republic, Manuel Ordía in Peru, Marcos Pérez Jiménez in Venezuela. So naturally, Guevara fled to the other camp—the Soviet Union and its unyielding leader Josef Stalin.

Short of money, the two travelers headed up to the leper colony to find work. But the horses that had been given to them had been taken from some Indians. Guevara gave them back and they proceeded on foot. At the leper colony, the constant rain precipitated an asthma attack and they had to leave. Staying in an opulent hacienda, the owner told them how he would invite poor families onto his land. But once they had cleared it and reaped their first harvest, he would move them on—this way getting his land cleared for free. He gave them horses, but the Indian servants he sent with them to carry their bags had to walk.

Guevara wrote: 'For the rich people of the region, it is completely natural for a servant to carry anything heavy and bear any discomfort, even though he is traveling on foot.'

Once out of sight of the landowner, they took their own bags. But the Indians, rather than thanking them, gave them a blank stare.

Further along, they stayed in a barracks that doubled as a prison. But the atmosphere turned sour after Guevara protested when one of the guards fondled a woman who had brought food for her imprisoned husband. Fortunately a lorry came by soon after and gave them a lift.

Now destitute, the two travelers developed a routine to get themselves food. First, they would speak loudly in exaggerated Argentine accents to attract a potential patron. This usually started a conversation. While one of them would outline their plight in a soft voice, staring into the distance, the other would mention loudly that this was the anniversary of the beginning of their trip. Granado would then let out a terrible sigh and announce: 'What a shame to be in this condition, since we can't celebrate it.'

When offered a drink, they said that they could not possibly accept as they could not reciprocate, then gave in. After that, Guevara would refuse another one, while Granado made fun of him. When the buyer grew insistent, Guevara then shamefacedly revealed that it was the Argentine custom to eat while drinking.

They frequently went without food and often found it difficult to find a place to stay. Guevara also had the problem of finding water and fire so he could sterilize his syringe. Sometimes he would have to inject himself with adrenaline, or whatever else was available, several times a day and his asthma attacks laid him up for days on end.

In Lima, they met Dr Hugo Pesce, who had set up a number of leper colonies they had visited. He arranged for them to stay in a lepers' hospital, while his assistant fed them and washed their clothes. Pesce was a writer, an intellectual and a leading member of the Peruvian Communist Party. He led the kind of highly principled life that Guevara himself aspired to. Later Che would send him a copy of his first book *Guerrilla Warfare*, with the dedication: 'To Doctor Hugo Pesce, who, without knowing it perhaps, provoked a great change in my attitude toward life and society, with the same adventurous spirit as always, but channeled toward goals more harmonious with the needs of America.'

Dr Pesce paid for a boat trip up the Ucayali River. On board was a pretty young prostitute whose services they paid for with accounts of the travels, much to the disapproval of the nuns. This brought back thoughts of Chichina. After a fortnight in another of Pesce's leper colonies, they took a raft down the Amazon. The disease was everywhere and Guevara was both horrified and fascinated by it.

He wrote to his mother, saying: 'One of the most interesting spectacles we have seen so far: an accordian player who had no fingers on his right hand, replacing them with some sticks tied to his wrist; the singer was blind and almost all of them were hideously deformed due to the nervous form of the disease found in this area… it looked like a scene from a horror movie.'

In Colombia, they were struck by the oppressive nature of the regime, which had taken over in a coup in 1948. Fidel Castro had been there at the time and had taken up arms against the new government, escaping via the Cuban embassy when the uprising was crushed. By the time Guevara turned up, a bloody clampdown, known simply as *La Violencia*, was underway.

After a run-in with the police, Guevara was searched. Asked about his inhaler, he said: 'Be careful, it is a very dangerous poison.'

He was arrested for 'making fun of the authorities.'

Released after several days, the two travelers followed the advice they had been given and quickly moved on to Venezuela. There, for the first time, Guevara wondered how black people, the descendants of slaves who he had previously had little to do with, fitted into his vision of an ethnically united *mestizo* Latin America. However, as with the Indians, he was more concerned with their lack of hygiene.

'The blacks... have maintained their racial purity thanks to their scant affection for bathing,' he wrote. He went on, condescendingly: 'The black is indolent and fanciful, he spends his money on frivolity and drink, while the European has a tradition of hard work and thrift.'

His racist attitudes did not change much when he got to Africa.

While Granado stayed in Venezuela to earn money in a leprosarium so they could continue their travels, Guevara headed home, hitching a ride on the plane of one of his rich friends that was taking race horses to Miami. Guevara says little about his month-long stopover in Florida while the plane was being fixed—his only visit to the US except for a week in 1964 attending the United Nations General Assembly. He did, however, say to the Argentinean journalist who helped him get a visa, 'I'd rather be an illiterate Indian than an American millionaire.'

Sadly, Guevara believed that all Latin Americans agreed with him, though the vast majority would have rather been an American millionaire than an illiterate Indian.

In Miami, Guevara tried to earn money by cleaning the apartment of a Cuban airline stewardess. But, having been brought up with maids and servants, he did not know how to clean and left the flat dirtier than he had found it. Guevara told Tita Infante: 'Those were the hardest and most bitter days of my life.'

Guevara's friend Jimmy Roca did not remember it that way. They spent every day on the beach, or sightseeing around the city. They did not talk politics, according to Roca, but just tried to enjoy themselves, drinking beer and eating French fries.

Chapter Four—The Romance of Revolution, 1953-1954

Guevara returned to Buenos Aires just five days after Eva Perón had died of cancer. She lay in state for two weeks and the country was in the grip of an unprecedented display of mourning. There, he saw Chichina again. They gazed at each other longingly, but her attitude was cold and distant; his talk was full of 'Yankee imperialism.' Besides, Guevara was busy elsewhere. He had passed sixteen of his medical examinations before he had left, but he had another fourteen to pass, which he intended to do in a year. He had to do this as, the following year, students would have to receive a 'political education' in *justicialismo*— the official name for Perónism—to graduate. As it was, he had to appear before the conscription board again. This time, he took no chances. He showered in freezing water beforehand to bring on an asthma attack.

Meanwhile, he took a little time out to write up his trips. In a foreword, he wrote rather self-consciously: 'The person who wrote these notes died the day he stepped back onto Argentine soil. The person who edits and polishes them, me, is no longer me; at least not the me I was before. Wandering around through our "America" has changed me more than I thought.'

He moved in with his Auntie Beatriz and worked fourteen hours a day. His studies made him ill. Grinding diseased human viscera without a protective mask, he had contracted an infection and was ordered to his bed. Nevertheless, he got up the next morning to sit an exam. By

December, he had passed the fourteen courses required and on July 12, 1953 he received his MD. His name even appeared on a paper in the scientific quarterly, *Alergia*, entitled 'Sensibilitization of Guinea Pigs to Pollens through Injections of Orange Extract' and he was offered a well-paid research job. However, he was soon off on his travels again.

Less than a month after graduating he boarded a train with his childhood friend Calica Ferrer on his way to Venezuela via Bolivia—though his ultimate goal was India. At Belgrano station, his mother ran along the platform in tears as the train left. She knew that she was losing her son forever.

*

In La Paz, Guevara became enamored of the Nationalist Revolutionary Movement led by Victor Paz Estenssoro, who had seized power the year before. He wrote to Tita Infante: 'Bolivia is a country which has given a really important example to America… Here revolutions are not done as they are in Buenos Aires… the government is supported by the armed people so there is no possibility of its being overthrown by an armed movement from abroad; it can only succumb to its own internal struggles.'

Again Guevara was appalled by the conditions in the mines. At one, the supervisors had shot down strikers with a machine gun. Guevara turned down a job working as a medical assistant in the mines and, rather than spend their time with the revolutionaries, Guevara and Ferrer moved out of their dingy hotel and into the home of a wealthy Argentine family. They socialized with Isaías Nogues, a sugar baron exiled by Péron and a Venezuelan General who would provide their visas for Venezuela. Nogues' playboy son Gobo, a friend of Aristotle Onassis, showed them around the town. They ate in the best restaurants and romanced a couple of rich girls, though Ernesto was shocked to see men snorting cocaine in the restroom.

Guevara soon became disillusioned with the revolution on the meager grounds that Indians visiting the presidential palace with their grievances were dusted down with DDT. Ernesto thought this humiliating, while Ferrer thought it practical as they were crawling with lice. On reflection, Guevara realized that the revolution was doomed. Although the new government had nationalized the mines, the United States was still their only customer and the US, with massive stockpiles built up during World War II, could control mineral prices worldwide. The administration had no other choice than to come to terms with the US.

While Guevara was there, the US envoy Milton Eisenhower, brother of the president, arrived to sign a trade agreement. In exchange for compensating the US mine owners, this pact preserved many of the regime's reforms and strengthened ties between the US military and Guevara's nemesis, the Bolivian Army. Guevara left no record of his views on this agreement.

Having bid farewell to their sweethearts, the two travelers headed for Peru. At the border, two of Guevara's books, *Man in the Soviet Union* and a publication of the Bolivian Ministry for Peasant Affairs, were confiscated on the grounds that they were 'Red.' They traveled on to Cuzco, a city so filthy that, according to Ferrer, '*El Chacho* bathed once and, by mutual agreement, for health purposes only'. Ferrer, whose aim was to live the good life in Venezuela after earning a fortune in the oil boom there, was not impressed. However, on the three-day bus trip to

Lima, Guevara delighted in bathing in the cold waters of a river beside a rest-stop and jumped up and down to wave to the shocked female passengers at the roadside.

In Lima, they stayed in the leprosarium again, but Gobo Nogues turned up and took them to the Country Club and the Gran Hotel Bólivar. Guevara met Dr Pesce again, but after they were arrested, apparently mistaken for two wanted kidnappers, and their room was turned upside down. To avoid any further problems he decided to avoid the doctor as he was under surveillance. Convinced that they were being harassed for being 'Reds,' Guevara and Ferrer headed for Ecuador by bus. His mother had written saying that she had arranged for the president to put them up. However, when they went to see him, they were told that President Velasco Ibarra could not see them. By now they had run out of all the money they had borrowed in Buenos Aires and Guevara imposed a strict regime of thrift.

Stuck in the banana port of Guayaquil, he hung around with other penniless exiles. He told a friend Andro Herrero that this was the first time he had felt true comradeship—off the rugby pitch at least. Herrero was shocked by Guevara's asthma attacks, which sometimes left him too weak to reach for his medicine. He volunteered to give Guevara the fare to Caracas, where he said he aimed to make enough money, working in the leprosarium with Alberto Granado, to send his mother to Paris for cancer treatment. Instead, after a couple of weeks, he decided to travel to Guatemala, along with his new-found friends. There, a leftist revolution under Jacobo Arbenz Guzmán threatened to nationalize the interests of the United Fruit Company and other US interests. 'There were', he said, 'four new candidates for Yankee opprobrium.' At the time, with the exception of Guetamala, Guevara maintained that the countries of Central America were 'not true nations, but private *estancias*,' run by US-backed dictators who were each condemned as flies in Pablo Neruda's poem 'The United Fruit Co.'

He said in December 1953: 'Along the way, I had the opportunity of traveling through the domains of the United Fruit Company, confirming once again the terrible nature of these capitalist octopuses. I have sworn before a picture of our old, much lamented comrade Stalin [who had died eight months before] that I will not rest until I see these capitalist octopuses annihilated.'

Nevertheless, Guevara sailed on a United Fruit Company ship to Panama. To pay off his rent arrears, he sold off everything except his books and his camera—what he called: 'The bourgeois remnants of my proprietorial hunger.' Even then Andro Herrero had to stay behind as surety. The normally reserved Guevara 'cried like a child' when Herrero saw him off on the dockside. He would never see Herrero or Ferrer again.

In Panama, he wrote a number of articles, one of which condemned the Americans for looting Machu Picchu of its archaeological treasures, even though it was an American, Professor Hiram Bingham, who rediscovered the lost city in 1911. This did not matter to Guevara. For him, Macchu Picchu was a political symbol.

'Let us agree, for now, that the [Inca] city may have two possible meanings,' he said. 'For the fighter… it is an arm stretched out to the future and a voice of stone with continental reach, shouting out: "Citizens of Indoamerica, reconquer the past!" For others… there is a sentence left in the hotel visitor book by a British subject which conveys all the bitterness of his nostalgia for empire: "I am lucky to find a place without a Coca-Cola propaganda." '

His anti-American sentiments were controversial since Panama was very much under American control. The US still owned the Canal Zone and there were several military bases there. However, he found a mentor, the Marxist ideologist Dr Carlos Moreno, at Panama University.

*

Guevara's father, concerned that his doctor son had pawned his suit in Guayaquil, sent respectable new clothes from Buenos Aires. Ernesto sold the lot for $100. This soon went as he was delayed for a month waiting for a visa to enter Costa Rica. Then, he hitchhiked out of Panama with a friend with $5 in his pocket, getting into a traffic accident on the way.

At the United Fruit Company's banana port Golfito, he took a ship named *Rio Grande*—though everyone called it *Pachuca* because it transported *pachucos* or 'down-and-outs'. Everyone was seasick except for Guevara, now a seasoned sailor, who amused himself 'with a negress who had picked me up—Socorro, as horny as a toad, with sixteen years spent on her back.'

In the Costa Rican capital of San José, he met a number of exiled Communist leaders who condemned the regime of Fulgencio Batista in Cuba. Among them were two survivors of the insurrection in Santiago de Cuba on July 26, 1953, Calixto García and Severino Rossel. They told him about their charismatic leader Fidel Castro, but Guevara was skeptical.

*

Cuban dictator Fulgencio Batista was the son of an impoverished farmer. He joined the army in 1921 and in September 1933 he organized the 'sergeant's revolt', which toppled the provisional government of Carlos Manuel de Cespedes, who had recently replaced the previous dictator Gerardo Machado y Morales. Rather than taking power himself, Batista controlled a series of civilian puppet presidents while pulling the strings in the background as army chief of staff. Then in 1940, he was elected president himself. He began a huge program of public works and greatly expanded the economy. He allowed the Mafia, controlled by New York gangster Meyer Lansky, to run the casinos there. Cuba became a resort island for the United States, famed for its music, cigars, rum and relaxed attitude to prostitution. Batista enriched himself with kickbacks and, at the end of his first presidential term in 1944, retired to Florida as a wealthy man. In 1952, he returned to Cuba, seizing power once more in a bloodless coup. Two years later, he was confirmed in office by popular elections and was re-elected again in 1958. However, his second period in office was marked by brutal repression, with Batista controlling the press, the universities and the Congress with an iron fist. Meanwhile, he embezzled huge sums from the overheating economy. The widespread corruption led to the growth of a guerrilla movement under Castro. Batista's flagrant abuse of power led to US President Dwight D. Eisenhower banning the sale of arms to Cuba. Without American backing, Batista could not resist Castro's forces and on 1 January 1959, he fled to the Dominican Republic. He lived comfortably in exile on the island of Madeira and in Estoril, near Lisbon, dying in Marbella, Spain on August 6, 1973.

*

In San José in 1953, Guevara also met the left-wing social reformer Rómulo Betancourt, who had been president of Venezuela from 1945 to 1948—and who would be again from 1958 to 1964, when guerrillas backed by Che tried to overthrow him. Ernesto asked him: 'If there was a war between the United States and the USSR, which side would you take?'

When Betancourt replied Washington, Guevara branded him a traitor on the spot.

From San José, Guevara drove to Guatemala City, arriving on New Year's Eve 1953 with $3. Although the Guatemalan government was backed by the Communists, the president, Jacobo Arbenz, was a moderate. However, finding its interests threatened, the US tarred him with the same brush. Spruille Braden gave a fiery speech at Dartmouth College denouncing him as a Communist and the CIA began training Guatemalan exiles in neighboring Honduras and El Salvador. Meanwhile hundreds of Latin American leftists rallied to the defense of Arbenz's 'socialist experiment.'

Guevara met other veterans of Castro's abortive July 1953 coup there including Ñico López, who had recently arrived in the city and brought fresh news from Cuba. This time, the Cubans and their talk of Castro impressed him. It was they who gave him the nickname 'Che.' It is a pseudonym often given to Argentinians. There are a large number of Italians in Argentina and Argentinians often pepper their speech with the Italian interjection 'che'—'what?'—although it is used in the way Americans of that era used 'Mac' or 'Bud.' Another theory is that it originated from Guaraní, the language of the Indians of northern Argentina, and means 'hey you'. There was another Cuban exile living in same hostel as Guevara, called José Manuel Vega Suárez, who was known as 'Che-Che'. Anyway, it was in Guatemala in the company of Cubans that 'Che' Guevara was born.

*

Guatemala is the largest and most populous of the Central American nations. It has coasts on the Pacific and the Caribbean, is bordered to the south by Honduras and El Salvador and to the north by Mexico and Belize—then known as British Honduras. In 1954, it had a population of three million, largely marginalized Indians. Its plantation economy was based on cotton, coffee and bananas. The social conditions were appalling. With the exception of Bolivia, it had the worst rates of urban and rural unemployment and underemployment in Latin America. The life expectancy of its people was the lowest in the region.

*

Che now drew inspiration from another Marxist, possibly an exile from Stalin's terror, who said: 'The future belongs to the people and, little by little or in one fell swoop, they will seize power, here and in the whole world. The bad thing is that they have to become civilized, and this can't happen before, but only after, taking power. They will become civilized only by learning at the cost of their own errors, which will be serious ones and which will cost many innocent lives.'

Indeed throughout Che's subsequent errors a great many innocent lives were spent.

In Guatemala, Guevara had decided to 'perfect' himself and 'achieve what I need to be an authentic revolutionary.' When his father offered to wire him money, he wrote back: '…even if I am dying I am not going to ask you for dough." And he advises his father to take the money he was going to spend on the telegram and buy a drink with it as 'I'm not going to answer any telegram of that type from now on.'

He tried to get a job at the ministry of health, but the minister turned him down. Guevara was bitter. He wrote to his mother, saying: 'The son-of-a-bitch who was supposed to hire me made me wait for a month, only to inform me he couldn't.'

The reason, apparently, was that he was not a card-carrying member of the Communist Party.

He was rescued from penury by Hilda Gadea, a Peruvian radical who was working for the Instituto de Fomento de la Producción and later became his first wife. She was three-and-a-half years older that him, short and plump—'a stocky girl with almond eyes, but ugly, quite ugly,' according to other Peruvian militants who knew the couple. Photographs bear this out. Even Ernesto thought so.

'I had a lot of asthma, if not I might have fucked her,' he wrote. 'I warned her that all I could offer her was casual contact, nothing definitive. She seemed very embarrassed. The little letter she left me upon leaving is very good, too bad she is so ugly.'

According to Hilda, the relationship was only consummated in Mexico the following May. But she was of mixed blood and that appealed to him, politically.

Hilda was not much impressed by Che either.

'On our first meeting, Guevara made a negative impression on me,' she said. 'He seemed too superficial to be an intelligent man, egotistical and conceited.'

However, she lent him money, nursed him through asthma attacks, and they discussed politics and philosophy. Both had a passion for existentialism and the works of Jean Paul Sartre. She also lent him a copy of Mao Tse-tung's *New China*. Meanwhile, he was having a secret fling with a nurse named Julia Mejía, a lapse he eventually confessed to Hilda.

Hilda lined him up a job, but to take it he would have to join the Guatemalan Communist Party. He refused. Instead, he made a little money translating for the American Marxist professor, Harold White, who he dismissed as a '*gringo*.' Eventually, after a period of selling encyclopedias, he undertook physical labor unloading tar barrels for a construction crew. This made him very proud. He was now part of the proletariat. It did not last long and he soon got a job in a laboratory at the Ministry of Sanitation.

In June, an armed column under Colonel Castillo Armas invaded the country and, under pressure from the US, President Arbenz resigned. Che was appalled. He thought Arbenz should have fought it out although—despite later propaganda issuing from Havana—he did not take up arms himself. He himself claimed to have 'tried to organize a group of young men like myself to confront the adventures of United Fruit.' In fact, many people suspected him of being a Perónist agent. But although he did not fight back, Guevara was thrilled to find himself under fire for the first time.

'I'm a bit ashamed to admit that I enjoyed myself immensely in those days,' he wrote. 'That magical sense of invulnerability... made me smack my lips with glee when I saw people running like crazy when they saw the planes... It was a lot of fun, what with the shooting, bombs, speeches and other distractions to break the monotony I was living in.'

Evidently he was a thrill-seeker and he blamed the newspapers for Arbenz's downfall.

'Too much freedom was given, there was even freedom for conspirators and agents of imperialism to destroy that democracy,' he told a fellow would-be revolutionary.

However, in an article he wrote called 'I Saw the Fall of Jacobo Arbenz,' he said that the real culprit was, as ever, 'Yankee imperialism.' And he knew where Arbenz had gone wrong. He wrote to Tita Infanta saying: 'There should have been a few firing squads early on … if those shootings had taken place the government would have retained the possibility of fighting back.'

It was a lesson he took to heart and later, when he had the chance, put into practice.

Guevara enjoyed the coup, but with the fall on the Arbenz regime Hilda was arrested and he sought asylum in the Argentine embassy. This brought him to the attention of the CIA for the first time. He became a committed Communist while locked up in the hothouse atmosphere of the embassy garage with twelve other troublemakers.

After a month, Che obtained a visa to visit Mexico, leaving Hilda behind without a passport after 'a profusion of fondles and a superficial screw.' There he got a job in a hospital and supplemented his earnings by taking pictures of American tourists and covering the Pan-American games for an Argentine news agency. He itched to try out his 'unrealized artistic ambition of becoming an actor' in the booming Mexican movie industry. He described this period as 'my proletarian life'—though he was clearly a rich boy slumming it.

He also cleaned up his act.

'I cook for myself and bathe every day,' he wrote to his mother. However, he did not wash his clothes much as he did not have the money for the laundry. He also outlined a book called *The Physician's Latin America*. The one constant in his life remained his anti-American sentiments.

'Mexico is entirely given over to the Yankees,' he wrote to his father. 'The press says nothing at all… The economic situation is terrible, prices are going up at an alarming rate, and… all the labor leaders have been bought off and sign unfair contracts with the Yankee companies in return for suppressing strikes.'

He intended to stay in Mexico for six months, then go on to the US, Europe and the Soviet Union, maybe even China—planning, perhaps, to take a scholarship for post-graduate studies in a European university along the way. However, in his letters, he gloomily predicted a world war following the uncertainty in the Kremlin precipitated by Stalin's death on March 5, 1953. A long-time admirer of the 'Man of Steel,' he began signing his letters 'Stalin II.'

Despite his asthma he climbed the 17,000-foot Pico de Orizaba and the 18,000-foot Popocatépetl, where his Cuban companion suffered frostbite. In November 1954 Hilda re-entered his life after she had been deported from Guatemala. Again she supplied him with money and satisfied his 'urgent need for a woman who will fuck.' They married on August 18, 1955, when she fell pregnant, seemingly at Che's insistence.

One day that summer, Che bumped into Ñico López at the hospital. He introduced him to Raúl Castro, who had recently been released from jail in Cuba. Soon after, his brother Fidel arrived in Mexico to form the 26th of July Movement which would eventually overthrow the Batista government in Havana in 1959.

*

Like Guevara, Castro was a son of the bourgeoisie. Born August 13, 1926 near Birán, eastern Cuba, he was the illegitimate son of a wealthy sugar planter from Spain who bought him the best education money could buy. Brought up as a Roman Catholic, Castro attended a Jesuit boarding school. During his five years at the University of Havana's Law School, he became involved in Cuba's violent brand of student politics. He was accused of the murder of another student leader, although the charge was never proved.

He participated in the attempted invasion of the Dominican Republic in 1947 to overthrow the US-backed dictator Rafael Trujillo. The following year, he took part in urban riots in Bogotá, Colombia. In 1952, he stood as an *Ortodoxos*—the Cuban People's Party—candidate for the Cuban House of Representatives. However, the former president General Fulgencio Batista seized power again and cancelled the elections.

On July 26, 1953, Castro staged an abortive attack on the Moncada army barracks in Santiago de Cuba. His comrades were gunned down and he was arrested. At his trial, he attacked the repressive Batista government, concluding with the famous words: 'History will absolve me.'

He was sentenced to fifteen years, but was released in an amnesty in 1955 and fled to Mexico where he met Che Guevara and formed the revolutionary 26th of July Movement. In December 1956, they returned to Cuba in a small motor cruiser called *Granma*. The small landing force was strafed by Cuban planes. Most of them were killed. But he survived and, after three years fighting in the Sierra Maestra, rode into power at the head of a popular revolution. Although Castro called for the US to pledge $30 billion to make Latin America safe for democracy, he soon became an authoritarian, first installing himself as Cuban premier, then president, then party chief, forcing the opposition into exile.

Within months of taking power, he arrested some 4,500 anti-Castro suspects. They faced mass trials in 1960. Even then, Castro was not a Communist or an implacable enemy of the US like Che. In 1948, he had honeymooned in the US and even considered staying on to study at Columbia University. When he came to power in 1959, the US did not hesitate to recognize his regime. He visited Washington, D.C., and assured congressmen that he would maintain Cuba's mutual defense treaty with the US, and allowed America to keep its navy base at Guantanamo Bay, even supplying it with water and electricity. However, relations soon cooled when he began nationalizing American-owned sugar plantations. In February 1960, Castro signed a deal to sell sugar barred by the US to the Soviet Union. In September, he gave a four-hour speech to the United Nations General Assembly in New York, denouncing American 'monopolists' and 'imperialists,' and praising the Soviet Union.

It was only in 1961 that his *Ortodoxos* merged with the Communist Party of Cuba and he became the general secretary. He then began fomenting revolution in Africa and Latin America. Under President Eisenhower, the CIA began to train anti-Castro Cuban exiles. Castro's response was to seize all US assets in Cuba, including, eventually, the American embassy. President Kennedy imposed an embargo on Cuban goods. However, many Europeans saw Castro as a romantic figure with Britain being the first to break the US blockade.

In 1961, CIA-trained exiles staged an abortive invasion at the Bay of Pigs, which was easily repelled by Castro's forces. Castro responded by allowing the Soviets to install nuclear missiles on the island, precipitating the Cuban Missile Crisis. Kennedy claimed to have won this showdown when the Soviet Union agreed to withdraw nuclear missiles from Cuba. The Soviets also claimed to have won as the US was forced to withdraw nuclear missiles from Turkey. In the aftermath, the CIA tried unsuccessfully to assassinate Castro, employing a 'dirty tricks' division who dreamed up such ideas as poisoning his cigars and sprinkling depilatory powder in his diving mask. The idea was that if Fidel lost his famous beard, with it he would lose his support.

Rogue CIA agents even tried to involve the Mafia, who had lost their casinos in Havana. Exploiting Castro's well-known weakness for women, they sent one of his lovers, a young German woman named Marita Lorenz who was living in New York, to Havana to poison him. According to Marita, he knew she had come to kill him and handed her his revolver, but she could not pull the trigger. These bungled assassination attempts backfired. Lee Harvey Oswald, Jack Ruby and others involved in the assassination of President Kennedy were closely involved with dissident Cubans, as were the 'plumbers' who burgled the Democratic Nation Committee offices in the Watergate building in 1972.

With Che, he began to 'export the revolution.' In 1975, he sent troops to Angola and, in 1978, to Ethiopia. In 1980, he emerged as the leader of the non-aligned world, despite obvious Soviet backing. Despite assassination attempts and international isolation—especially after the collapse of the Soviet Union in 1991—Castro clung on to power, even introducing a dollar economy, reversing the policy of the previous thirty years when owning dollars was illegal. Meanwhile, his people risked almost anything to flee, the country decayed and in 2003 seventy-five dissidents were jailed for up to twenty-eight years for daring to speak out against the regime. They have concrete slabs for beds, eat food that would 'make a pig vomit' and use lavatories that 'regurgitate their fetid contents around the clock.' Until he stood down in 2008 in favor of his brother Raúl, he remained the world's longest surviving head of state.

Chapter Five—Becoming a Guerrilla, 1955-1956

Fidel Castro arrived in Mexico City on 8 July 1955. Che met him at the home of Cuban radical María Antonia and her husband the wrestler 'Dick' Merano. They talked for ten hours straight, from eight at night until the following morning. From then on, they saw each other almost every day.

'It is a political event to have met Fidel Castro, the Cuban revolutionary, a young man who is intelligent, very sure of himself and remarkably bold,' wrote Che in his journal. 'I think there is a mutual liking.'

Castro recalled ten years later that Che's 'revolution development was more advanced than mine, ideologically speaking. From the theoretical point of view he had a better background, he was more advanced as a revolutionary.'

The Venezuelan poet Lucila Velázquez who shared an apartment with Che and Hilda, and who later became Fidel's girlfriend, summed up the relationship: 'Fidel's passion for Cuba and Guevara's revolutionary ideas ignited each other like wildfire, in an intense flare of light. One was impulsive, the other thoughtful; one emotional and optimistic, the other cold and skeptical. One was attached only to Cuba; the other, devoted to a framework of social and economic concepts. Without Ernesto Guevara, Fidel Castro might never have become a Communist.

Without Fidel Castro, Ernesto Guevara might never have been more than a Marxist theoretician, an idealistic intellectual.'

They had a lot in common though. They both hated Yankees, particularly the United Fruit Company which also had large interests in Cuba. They were both sexually voracious and, curiously for a Cuban, and like Guevara, Castro could not dance. Both were the spoilt sons of comparatively wealthy families and they both believed that they were men of destiny.

On meeting Castro, Guevara noted: 'I met him during one of those cold Mexican nights, and remember that our first discussion was about world politics. After a few hours—by dawn—I had already embarked on my future expedition. Actually, after the experience I had had walking through all Latin America and the finishing touch in Guatemala, it wasn't hard to talk me into joining any revolution against a tyrant, but Fidel impressed me as an extraordinary man. He faced and resolved the most impossible things… I shared in his optimism. There was a lot to do, to fight for, to plan. We had to stop crying and start fighting.'

As well as discussing Batista's Cuba, they soon found themselves talking of the fall of Perón which occurred in September 1955. Naturally, Che put this down to American interference which was almost certainly not true.

Through Raúl Castro, Che also met Nikolai Leonov, a KGB agent who had traveled to Mexico to learn Spanish and would be a key link between Moscow and the Cuban revolution. Che remained a committed Stalinist. Learning Russian in the Mexican-Soviet Institute of Cultural Relations in Mexico City, he denounced Nikita Khrushchev's condemnation of Stalin at the 20th Party Congress in Moscow as imperialist propaganda. He supported the Soviet crushing of the 1956 Hungarian Uprising, claiming that 'the Budapest insurrection was a fascist conspiracy against the people.'

Leonov was impressed by Guevara and his commitment to the cause, and recalled: 'Che looked very well, radiant with happiness because here was a representative of the other world, of the Socialist camp, and we began discussing everything. He asked me about the Soviet Union because in that year, 1956, a great many things had happened. He was basically well-informed, though concrete matters such as the Central Committee meetings, did not interest Che. He knew a lot about the Soviet Union, how the society was structured, how the economy functioned, that is, he had a basic understanding of what was then the Soviet Union. At the time everybody had the same vision, the same admiration. He was an admirer [of the Soviet Union].'

Castro encouraged Che to take Hilda on their honeymoon to southeast Mexico, where they saw the Mayan ruins. Che wrote a poem commemorating the long-dead 'Latin American' people who had built them, complete with the obligatory swipe at '*gringo* tourists.' Much to his chagrin, Che himself was mistaken for a *gringo* going out with a Mexican woman when he and Hilda visited a bar in Veracruz. This nearly provoked a fight.

The newly-weds had a couple of rows on the trip—one when he refused to let her give him an adrenalin injection; another when he made fun of her and other passengers who got seasick on the voyage home. However, on the trip he did manage to procure several bagfuls of *yerba maté* to which by then he was addicted.

'He was never without his equipment, the *bombilla* [the silver straw that maté is sucked through], *boquilla* [the mouthpiece], and a two-liter thermos of hot water,' Hilda wrote. 'Studying, conversing, he always drank maté; it was the first thing he did when he got up and the last thing he did before going to sleep.'

When they returned to Mexico City, training for the invasion of Cuba had started. It began easily enough with long walks along the Avenida Insurgents and rowing on the lake in Chapultepec Park. Diet and exercise were supervised by the Mexican wrestler Arzacio 'Kid' Venegas. Che cut out the steak that he usually had for breakfast to keep his weight down. Later, they went out to the Santa Rosa ranch near the town of Chalco.

As early as September 1955, Che announced his intention to die fighting in the Caribbean. However, he told his mother that he wanted to continue traveling 'as long as necessary to complete my education and give myself the pleasures I have allotted myself in my life project.' As late as March the following year, he was still talking about obtaining a scholarship to study in France. Indeed Che had considered the possibility of victory in Cuba 'very doubtful.' Landing a band of guerrillas on Cuba's well-defended coast-line seemed a crazy idea, but Che supported Castro nonetheless.

Hilda noticed that the normally talkative Che fell silent in Castro's company and began calling Fidel his 'controller.' But then, few could get a word in edgeways when Castro was talking. Hilda once asked Castro, if the struggle was in Cuba, why he was in Mexico? The answer lasted four hours.

A few days later Che told Hilda that he was going to Cuba with Castro. This was a special privilege. Che was the only foreigner Castro allowed in his revolutionary band and bolstered his confidence by making him head of personnel. This did not make '*el Argentino*' popular with the Cubans who disliked his self-righteousness. The latter showed itself when the Moncada-veteran Melba Hernández arrived from Havana and he told her that she could not be a revolutionary because she wore too much jewelry.

'Real revolutionaries adorn themselves on the inside, not on the surface,' he said.

But Castro rallied to Guevara's defense.

'About twenty or thirty Cubans … challenged Che's leadership because he was an Argentine,' he said. 'We of course criticized this attitude … this ingratitude toward someone who, although not born in our land, was ready to shed his blood for it. And I remember the incident hurt me a great deal. I think it hurt him as well.'

They celebrated Christmas together with the traditional Cuban dish 'Moors and Christians'—black beans with rice—and, on February 15, Hilda gave birth. Che was disappointed. He had wanted a son who he planned to call 'Vladimiro Ernesto'— Vladimir for Lenin, of course. Instead, he had a daughter who was Christened Hildita, but Che called her 'little Mao' as she had inherited narrow oriental eyes from her mother.

'The offspring is really ugly,' he wrote to his mother. 'The only thing that differentiates her immediately from any other baby: her papa is Ernesto Guevara.'

He soon explained to Hilda that they must both make sacrifices for the revolution, the first of which would be prolonged separation. He went to Santa Rosa training school, telling her that he might not be back.

On June 24, 1956, at the urging of Batista, Castro was arrested. He took the police to Santa Rosa, where he persuaded the rest of his men to surrender. Even Hilda and the baby were detained overnight. Some of the men were tortured by being plunged naked and bound into freezing water and repeatedly submerged until they were on the point of drowning. Then they were interrogated by a masked man with a Cuban accent. However, Castro soon managed to persuade the Mexican authorities to release his men—with the exception of Che who had overstayed his tourist visa.

In fact, the authorities already had a considerable file on him because of his visits to the Mexican-Soviet Institute and to the Soviet embassy to borrow books from Leonov. He even sat in on meetings of the Mexican Communist Party. Finding Leonov's business card in his pocket, the authorities accused Guevara of being a spy.

Che told Castro not to waste time and money trying to get him out:

'The revolution should not be impeded on my account,' he said.

Fidel replied: 'I will not abandon you.'

'Those personal attitudes of Fidel, with people he appreciates, are the key to that fanaticism he awakens in others,' Che wrote later.

This is the only time Che would ever spend in jail—until the eve of his execution—and he maintained throughout that he was a hard-line pro-Soviet Communist revolutionary.

While Castro told his interrogator that he was a follower of the father of Cuban independence José Martí, Guevara admitted openly that he was a Marxist-Leninist and even took on the public prosecutor in an ideological debate.

'Because Che was being very arrogant, with all the weight of his knowledge, he was winning the entire discussion in an ideological debate that was completely irrelevant,' said Gutiérrez Barrios, an agent at the Mexican Federal Security Directorate.

The other detainees tried to hide their political affiliations, but Guevara actually tried to convert his captors. This infuriated Castro. He always played the nationalist whose only aim was to introduce Western democracy to Cuba because any hint of Communist backing would lead the Eisenhower administration to increase their support for Batista's regime.

Guevara was unrepentant. He wrote to his mother from jail: 'I am not Christ or a philanthropist, old lady, I am the total opposite of Christ… I fight for the things I believe in, with all the weapons at my disposal and try to leave the other man dead so that I don't get nailed to the cross… What terrifies me is your lack of comprehension of all this and your advice about moderation, egoism, etc… that is to say, all of the most execrable qualities an individual can have. Not only am I not a moderate, I shall not ever try to be one, and when I recognize that the sacred flame within me has given way to a timid votive light, the least I could do is to vomit over my own shit.'

He went on to condemn her call to moderate self-interest as 'rampant and dreadful individualism.'

He claimed that during his time in prison and his days of training, he had begun to identify totally with his comrades and the cause.

'The concept of 'I' disappeared totally to give place to the concept "us",' he said.

As a Communist, he naturally felt that it was 'beautiful to be able to feel that removal of I.' He signed the letter with his new nom de guerre 'Your son, El Che.'

At the same time as writing this explosive letter to his mother, he was penning what amounts to almost a love poem to Castro called '*Canto a Fidel.*' It begins:

Let's go, ardent prophet of the dawn

Along remote and unmarked paths

To liberate the green caiman you so love…

When the first shot sounds

And in virginal surprise the entire jungle awakens

There, at your side, serene combatants

You'll have us.

After fifty-five days in jail, Che was released on the condition that he left the country within a few days. He spent three days at home with his wife and daughter, then, on Castro's orders, he left the capital and checked into a hotel at Ixtapal de la Sal under a false name. This was something of a relief. Che wrote that the arrival of his daughter had 'put an end to a disastrous conjugal situation.'

He went on: 'My incapacity to live with her mother is greater than my affection for her. For a moment I thought that a combination of the little girl's charm and consideration for her mother (who is in many ways a great woman, who loves me in an almost pathological way) might turn me into a boring family man. Now I know this will not be the case, and that I will pursue my bohemian life until who knows when.'

This is how he explained his absence to his six-month-old baby daughter. He held her in his arms one day and said: 'My dear daughter, my little Mao, you don't know what a difficult world you're going to have to live in. When you grow up this whole continent, and maybe the whole world, will be fighting against the great enemy, Yankee imperialism. You too will have to fight. I may not be here anymore, but the struggle will enflame the continent.' Overhearing this, Hilda went over and hugged him.

While Castro publicly renounced violence, training now began in earnest. He had received $50,000 from Carlos Prío, the former president of Cuba that Batista had ousted who was now living in exile in the US. However, it is thought that the money really came from the CIA. The US was becoming increasingly disillusioned with Batista, and Castro, in his public pronouncements at least, was a moderate reformer and constitutionalist. Only Che was a Communist.

With the money, Castro bought the ranch and a number of safe houses, and he employed Alberto Bayo, a former Republican general from the Spanish Civil War to train the men. They were now training with live ammunition, shooting turkeys so they could practice on moving targets. Che excelled. According to Bayo's report he was 'an excellent with approximately 650 bullets [fired]. Excellent discipline, excellent leadership qualities, excellent physical stamina. Some disciplinary press-ups for small errors in interpreting orders and faint smiles.'

Although he was supposed to be joining the expedition as a doctor, with Bayo's encouragement, Che began to take a leadership role.

However, on a long route march, with poor provisions and excessive discipline, the Cubans rebelled against the leadership of the Argentinian and the Spaniard. Che ordered a court-martial and a death sentence was passed. It is thought that at least one—perhaps three—men were executed for indiscipline while training. It was the beginning of Guevara's murderous career.

Castro bought a thirty-eight-foot motor launch called *Granma* from an American expatriate called Robert Erickson for $15,000. It was neither seaworthy nor big enough. As part of the deal, Castro also had to buy Erickson's riverside house at Tuxpan on the Gulf coast. There, Castro's men began mending the yacht. Meanwhile, in a raid on a safe house in Mexico City, the police seized twenty rifles and 50,000 rounds of ammunition. Nevertheless, Che and the others assembled at Tuxpan.

Castro's agents in Cuba, who were supposed to stir up uprisings to coincide with the landings, told him that they were not ready. Furthermore the Cuban Communist Party told him to abandon his invasion plan and join them in a gradual build-up to an armed insurrection. But Castro was determined to go ahead. He had often repeated the pledge: 'In 1956 we will be free or we will be martyrs.'

It was now November and Batista was expecting him. Indeed, the Cuban dictator's chief of staff had called a press conference to mock the ambitions of Castro as a revolutionary leader. Meanwhile, land and sea patrols were increased.

Before dawn on November 25, 1956, Castro's men scrambled on board the *Granma*. Not everyone had arrived. Others had to be left behind due to lack of space. The small boat carried forty light machine pistols, thirty-five rifles with telescopic sights, fifty-five regular

Mexican rifles, three Thompson machine guns, and two anti-tank guns. It was also loaded to the gunwales with food, water, and ammunition. And there were eighty-two men on board a boat designed to carry twenty. One of them was Ernesto 'Che' Guevara. Before they shoved off, he left behind a letter to be forwarded to his mother. It told her that 'the potatoes are really in the fire' and lamented his lack of knowledge of surgery which he would surely need to attend to wounded men.

'And now comes the tough part, old lady,' he wrote, 'from which I have never run away and have always liked. The skies have not turned black, the constellations have not come out of their orbits nor have there been floods or overly insolent hurricanes; the signs are good. They signal victory. But if they are mistaken, and in the end even the gods make mistakes, then I believe I can say like a poet you don't know: 'I will only take to my grave/the nightmare of an unfinished song.' I kiss you again, with all the love of a goodbye that resists being total. Your son.'

Chapter Six—Fighting in the Sierra Maestra, 1957–1958

Che Guevara was the expedition's medical officer and had been given the rank of lieutenant. He was inadequate to the task from the beginning. A number of the men became seasick almost as soon as they weighed anchor, but they found the ship's doctor floored by an asthma attack. He had neglected to bring with him any adrenaline or even an inhaler for himself—or any seasickness pills for the others.

Castro's supporters staged an uprising in Santiago de Cuba on November 30. A reception committee of a hundred men and trucks awaited him at the Cabo Cruz lighthouse at the easterly end of Cuba in the province of Oriente, in an area now renamed Granma. But the over-loading, the heavy seas, a defective motor, and poor navigation meant the *Granma* was seventy-two hours late. When it did arrive, the reception committee had gone home. The navigator fell overboard trying to spot the lighthouse. After they circled back to get him, they beached on a sandbar. Leaving behind most of their equipment, they struggled ashore in broad daylight. A coastguard cutter has already spotted them.

Inland was a mangrove swamp. The landing party was dispersed as Cuban planes fired at them with machine guns. It was two days before the survivors managed to regroup and were led out of the swamp by a local peasant. He took them to a place called Alegría de Pío where they bivouacked at the edge of a cane field, while he went to inform the army of the guerrillas' presence.

At 4.30 that afternoon, the bedraggled rebels were attacked. Castro fled into the forest. Ñico López, Che's first Cuban friend, was cut down. Some returned fire, or simply panicked, abandoning their equipment. Che had cooler head. But he had a decision to make. As he made for cover should he take with him a first-aid kit or a box of ammunition? He took the ammunition and decided then that he was no longer a doctor but a true revolutionary.

Seconds later he was hit by bullet. It knocked him to the ground and he was sure he was going to die. He grew strength from a story of Jack London's he remembered, where a man in the wastes of Alaska fails to light a fire and props himself up against a tree to die with dignity.

Although others suggested they surrender, Che and four comrades dragged themselves into the forest. The cane field behind them was soon on fire and planes in the sky fired down on them. That night they slept huddled together and in the morning they started traveling eastwards, toward the Sierra Maestra.

They had precious little food and water, though they gorged on prickly pears—the only foodstuff they could find. They picked up another three comrades along the way. The eight of them dodged planes and army patrols, sleeping where they could. Then one night, it desperation, they knocked a farmhouse door. The owner turned out to be a Seventh Day Adventist pastor who fed them. But they were in such bad condition that the food immediately prompted diarrhea.

'The little house that sheltered us turned into an inferno,' he wrote, 'in a flash, eight unappreciative intestines gave evidence of the blackest ingratitude.'

Local people told them that sixteen of the rebels had been killed, some shot after surrendering. Five were known to have been taken alive, while others, like themselves, were on the run. It was not known if Castro was among them.

The eight were spread out among surrounding houses. They shed their uniforms and weapons—all except for Che and one other who kept a pistol each. When they moved on, they found that they had been betrayed. The army found their weapons cache and took away a sick comrade who had been too ill to continue.

Then Guillermo García, a member of the 26 July peasant network, turned up and said that Fidel Castro—or 'Alejandro', as he was calling himself—and his brother Raúl were still alive. García lead them to his hideout. The meeting was not a happy one. Castro reproached them bitterly for having lost their weapons. The reproach hurt Che. His response was an asthma attack.

'For the duration of the campaign and even today [Fidel's] words remained engraved on my mind: "You have not paid for the error you committed, because the price you pay for the abandonment of your weapons under such circumstances is your life. The one and only hope of survival that you would have had, in the event of a head-on encounter with the army, was your guns. To abandon them was criminal and stupid." '

Che's asthma disappeared the following day when new weapons turned up. But Castro stripped Che of his officer's pistol, instead giving him a 'bad rifle.' The number of survivors from the *Granma*, who now formed the core of the revolutionary army, has traditionally been put at twelve. In fact, Che names fifteen, including himself, in his book

Reminiscences of the Cuban Revolutionary War, while other sources put the number as high as twenty-two.

The Batista government, naturally, claimed total victory. Listed among the dead were the Castro brothers and Ernesto Guevara. Hilda was devastated at the news. So were his mother and father—especially as his mother received the 'death or glory' letter he had left behind in Mexico soon after. But then they heard from the Argentine ambassador in Havana that he was not among the dead or wounded. In fact, the Cuban newspapers were soon writing about 'an Argentine Communist with terrible antecedents, expelled from his country' who was now part of Castro's revolutionary force. Che was delighted. Recognition at last.

A number of local peasants joined the original band—most of whom had now been made officers. They sought refuge in the Sierra Maestra, the mountainous region of southern Cuba, where rainforest still survived. There, Castro made an alliance with Crescencio Pérez, a local outlaw who was said to have killed several men and fathered eighty children in the Sierra. His extensive family provided vital manpower and Castro used them to maintain contact with the 26th of July movement in the cities. But while Castro was asking them for more weapons, Che was beseeching urban comrades to send books—particularly requesting books on algebra, Cuban history and geography, and French texts, as he was teaching Raúl the language.

Che accompanied Castro on a daring raid on barracks. They were lead into town by one of the local *mayorales* who mistook Castro for an officer in the *guardia rurales* and, when asked what they should do if they caught Castro, replied: 'Cut his balls off.' He was executed as soon as the firing started.

The raid netted food, weapons and ammunition. Che took a corporal's cap as a trophy, which he wore with pride. Later, mistaking him for the enemy, one of his own men fired on him. And on January 22, 1957, in the appropriately name Hell's Creek, Che killed his first enemy with his own hand.

In February, the veteran journalist Herbert Matthews of *The New York Times* turned up to interview Castro, who laid on the theatrics by having a sweating messenger burst in with an urgent dispatch from the 'second column'—implying they had more than the twenty or so men to hand. When Matthew's piece appeared in *The New York Times*, it was accompanied by a picture of Che sporting a gun and a scruffy beard. When Che's parents saw it, they were relieved. At last, they had confirmation that their son was alive.

'Now we knew that Ernesto was fighting for a cause that was recognized as just,' said his father, who turned his office in to the local branch of the 26th of July movement support committee. Meanwhile, Hilda, who had returned to Peru, opened a branch in Lima. She wrote to Che asking whether she could join him in the Sierra Maestra when Hildita was old enough. His reply, which took four or five months to reach her, said that she could not come yet as the fighting was at a dangerous stage. In fact, he already had another lover.

The New York Times article also prompted an attack on the presidential palace in Havana by other radical groups. The uprising was crushed but it sent more recruits out into the Sierra Maestra. Three Americans joined up, one was a runaway from the US Navy base at Guantánamo bay. However, other key supporters in the cities were arrested and other journalists and the US TV networks were soon on the trail of Castro's rebel army and Che sometimes acted as translator.

When Matthews had gone, it was discovered that their peasant guide Eutimio Guerra was a traitor. He had in his possession a safe-conduct pass from the army.

'Eutimio got down on his knees, asking to be shot and get it over with,' Che wrote. Castro and the others agreed he must die, but the identity of his executioner was a closely guarded secret until the biographer John Lee Anderson got access to Che's private diaries.

'The situation was uncomfortable for the people and for [Eutimio],' wrote Che, 'so I ended the problem giving him a shot with a .32 pistol in the right side of the brain, with an exit wound in the right side of the temporal lobe. He gasped a little and was dead...'

Then, Guevara recorded an unbelievable event: 'Proceeding to remove his belongings, I could not get the watch off which was tied to his belt by a chain, and then he told me in a steady voice farther away than fear: "Yank it off, boy, what does it matter..." So I did and his possessions are now mine. We slept badly, wet and I with something of asthma.' In fact, it was malaria.

Che did not mention taking the dead man's possessions in his published account of the event 'Death of a Traitor.' The execution gave Che a reputation of cold-bloodedness and many of his own men were afraid of him. Some deserted or wounded themselves so they would not have to fight alongside him. He refused their request to put a cross on the grave in case it gave their presence away. He did not seem to have been bothered by this in the slightest. The next day there was a visitor to their headquarters. 'She is,' wrote Che in his journal, 'a great admirer of the movement who seems to me to want to fuck more than anything else.'

Che was laid low by malaria in March, then by some rotten pork supplied by a peasant collaborator. This was followed by another asthma attack brought on by the humidity. He was left behind when he was unable to walk. But he managed to secure a supply of adrenaline from Manzanillo and by end of May his thirst for combat had returned. However, when he caught up with Castro, he turned down Che's plan for an attack on one of the mobile army units in the area. Che was to resume his position as the rebel army's doctor.

'Raúl tried to argue that I be made political commissar as well, but Fidel was opposed,' wrote Che.

He began holding open-air surgeries for the local peasants to win their favor, playing the people's doctor that he had once wanted to be, for the one and only time. Most thought that the presence of the rebels only brought the wrath of the army down on them. The rebels themselves resorted to banditry to survive—even stealing and eating a peasant's horse on one occasion. The peasants could not understand Castro's stated strategy of burning the sugar plantations that supplied at least some work come harvest time. Nevertheless, stepping up the economic war, Castro even ordered the burning of his own family's sugar plantation. But there were still plenty of peasants happy to betray them to the army. Castro would unmask them by pretending to be in the *guardias rurales* to win their confidence and Che was there to take care of business.

'The informer was executed,' wrote Che on April 15, 1957, 'ten minutes after giving him the shot in the head, I declared him dead.'

Che was keen on executing prisoners, though Castro tried to restrain him in the hope that some of Batista's army would defect. When asked whether capital punishment was really justified, Che argued that the guerrilla army had no other alternative in most cases and he never flinched when it came to the moment. He also authorized reprisal killings. However, as the war dragged on, he instituted fake executions, where the victim would have no idea that he was not really going to be shot. Although he admitted such punishment was barbaric but he saw no other alternative.

On May 28, 1957, the rebels attacked the barracks at Ulvero. Che was in the thick of the fighting. According to Castro: 'Che asked for three or four men and in a matter of moments started out to launch an attack from that direction.'

While one of Guevara's closest aides, Harry 'Pombo' Villegas said: 'He was a man who liked to take the lead in combat, to set an example; he would never say, go and fight, but rather, follow me into combat.'

When the garrison surrendered and the fighting was over, Che tended the wounded on both sides, though still ruing his lack of medical experience. This time, while the others looted weapons, Che took medical supplies. Fearing a counterattack by the army, Castro made off, leaving Che with a column of the wounded.

Carrying those too ill to walk into the forest on improvised stretchers made out of hammocks, Che nursed several of his men back to health. While some deserted, others joined his band. He even attempted a little dentistry on his charges, using what he called 'psychological anaesthesia'—that is, cursing his patients if they complained too much.

'I exercised my new profession with great enthusiasm,' he said. However, the results were not impressive.

Che's column reached Castro's headquarters on July 17, only to find that Fidel had signed the 'Sierra Pact' with two of the moderate mainstream parties. Che characterized this as a 'betrayal' and he accused Fidel's new-found friends of wanting 'to maintain the rule of imperialism in Cuba through its commercial bourgeoisie, which was tightly linked to Northern masters.'

They also pledged to compensate land-owners who suffered in their program of agrarian reform and to hold free elections after the fall of the current regime. However, Che insisted that the pact should be viewed as a short-term expedient that they could tear up later when it suited them.

Meanwhile, Che was promoted and given command of the second column of seventy-five men. It was designated Column No. 4 to give the enemy the impression that they were stronger than, in fact, was the case. He was enormously proud to be a *comandante*.

'The vanity which we all have in us made me the proudest man in the world that day,' he said.

His badge of rank, a small star, was supplied by Celia Sánchev, Fidel's lover and the rebels' contact in nearby Manzanillo. She also gave him a wristwatch.

The first thing he did as *comandante* was warn his men, over the unburied body of an executed comrade, that deserting or betraying the revolution would be punished by death. The body remained unburied on the Maestra.

'I am not very convinced of the legality of his death, although I used it as an example,' he said. 'The body was on its stomach, showing at a glance that it had a bullet hole in the left lung and had its hands together and fingers folded as if they were tied.'

Later, after a number of desertions, Che set up a disciplinary commission. For security reasons, the men were not even allowed to keep a diary—except Che, of course.

He led his men in an assault on the army garrison at Bueycito, where he was lucky to escape with his life after his Thompson machine gun jammed in a firefight and he had to 'run with a speed I have never matched since.' They killed six soldiers and took others prisoner. The government's response was to torture and kill rebel suspects, leaving their mutilated corpses hanging from trees or dumped by the roadside. Protest was brutally suppressed. This turned the US government against Batista and the State Department and the CIA gradually began to support Castro, tacitly at least, rejecting Batista's characterization of him as a Communist. US representatives even approached leaders of the 26th of July Movement and offered 'any kind of help in exchange for our ceasing to loot arms from their base' at Guantánamo. They even supplied a visa and passage out of the country for a representative to go fundraising in the States, while the CIA provided another $50,000 to support the cause. And when Batista used tanks, B-26s bombers and other US-supplied firepower against the rebels, the US administration pointed out that this was a violation of their defense treaty.

On August 29, Che's gallant little bunch held off 140 soldiers armed with bazookas, but later he learnt that the army had murdered a number of peasants in reprisal. Initially, Che killed soldiers his men had taken prisoner. But gradually, his attitude toward prisoners of war mellowed. He stopped his men killing them and gave them first aid. But he was never less than ruthless with his own men, executing them after being found guilty by a revolutionary tribunal. Many died while proclaiming their loyalty to the revolution. One, 'Squinty' Echeverria, died, Guevara recalled, after writing 'a long, moving letter to his mother, in which he explained the justice of his punishment and instructed her to remain loyal to the revolution.'

El Maestro—'the Teacher'—a guerrilla who had nursed Guevara through a bout of asthma, was shot after growing a beard and passing himself off as Che 'the doctor.' According to Castro *El Maestro* would announce to the peasants: 'Bring me women. I'm going to examine them all.'

'Did you ever hear of anything so outrageous. We shot him.' Castro wrote.

Che established his own stronghold, El Hombrito. There he started a guerrilla newspaper *El Cubano Libre*—'The Free Cuban'— which was run off on an old mimeograph machine. Che wrote a column under the sobriquet *El Francotirado*—'The Sniper'—praising the Soviet achievement of launching *Sputnik*, the first man-made satellite. Later he started a radio station, *Radio Rebelde*—'Radio Rebel.' He also constructed fortifications, air-raid shelters, a make-shift hospital, a farm, and an armory carrying rudimentary land mines and rifle-launched grenades also known as 'sputniks.' These were originally condensed milk tins packed with gunpowder, fired from scuba-divers' spear guns. They made a lot of noise but inflicted little damage. They even had a mascot, a puppy. However, when it followed them on an operation, Che ordered that it be killed.

Soon after, they were forced out of El Hombrito. Fighting a rear-guard action at Altros de Conrado on December 8, Che was shot in the left foot. The bullet had to be removed with a razor blade. Castro was concerned that Che was risking his own life and ordered him not to take on role in combat, but rather concern himself with directing operations.

Guevara wrote back: 'I am sorry to have disregarded your advice, but our people's morale was very low... and I considered my presence necessary in the line of fire.'

They retook El Hombrito, but all the facilities there had been destroyed. Early the following year, Che set up a new headquarters at El Mesa. This soon boasted a butcher's shop, a leather workshop and a cigar factory. By this time, like Castro, Che had become addicted to tobacco. He was becoming a Cuban, though he had not given up the yerba maté.

Now as a company commander, Che could at last take part in the debates and discussion in the 26th of July movement. While his position echoed that of Castro, he was consistently more radical and he grew an intense dislike for anyone he considered a reformist. When Cuban opposition groups signed a pact in Miami on November 1, 1957, Che condemned it, saying: 'In Miami they proffered their ass in the most despicable act of buggery that Cuban history is likely to recall.'

And he condemned those who supported the pact as 'rightist'—a capital crime in Guevara's eyes.

'In contrast, those who have your ideological training believe that the solution to our ills lies in liberating ourselves from a noxious Yankee domination by means of a no less noxious Soviet domination,' Che was told by René Ramos Latour.

Castro was silent on the matter. Che, now seen as the leader of the left, wrote to him saying that his silence was 'inadvisable.' However, Fidel had always wanted to wait until they were in power before they confronted the Americans.

'Unfortunately we have to face Uncle Sam before the time is ripe,' Che wrote, urging Castro to speak out against the Miami pact. Castro took his advice. He issued a communiqué saying: 'The leadership of the struggle against tyranny is, and will continue to be, in Cuba and in the hands of the revolutionary fighters.'

He then claimed that the 26th of July movement, alone, claimed the right to control Cuba after the fall of Batista.

'These are our conditions,' he said. 'If they are rejected, then we will continue the struggle on our own… To die with dignity does not require company.'

Che ran off copies of the statement on his mimeograph machine and, on February 2, 1958, *Bohemia*, the only uncensored magazine in Cuba, reproduced it in a special print run of 500,000 copies. Che was full of praise for Fidel

'Lenin already said it, the policy of principle is the best policy,' Guevara told Castro. 'The end result will be magnificent… Now you are on the even greater path of becoming one of the two or three in America who will have taken power through a multitudinous armed struggle.'

Che recognized that this move might cost Castro American support, but 'the people cannot be defeated.'

'Because of my ideological training I am one of those who believe that the solution to this world's problems is to be found behind the so-called Iron Curtain... I always viewed Fidel as a genuine leader of the bourgeois left, though his character is enriched by personal qualities of extraordinary brilliance which raise him far above his class. It is in that spirit that I joined the struggle...'

ERNESTO 'CHE' GUEVARA

Che now began to attract some press attention himself. *New York Times* correspondent Homer Bigart was sent to track him down. Bigart was accompanied by Uruguayan journalist Carlos María Gutiérrez and found Guevara 'very thin, with a sparse beard that barely framed an almost childlike face.'

'There were no orders given, nor permissions grants, nor military protocol,' wrote Gutiérrez, 'the guerrillas of La Mesa reflected a discipline that was more intimate, derived from the men's confidence in their leaders. Fidel, Che and the others lived in the same line as they did. Guevara didn't have to abandon his *porteños* [Buenos Airean] brusqueness to show that he loved them, and they paid him back with the same virile reticence, with an adherence that went deeper than mere obedience.'

The Argentine journalist Jorge Richardo Massetti was also unimpressed by 'the few hairs sprouting from his chin that wanted to be a beard,' adding dismissively that: 'The famous Che Guevara seemed to me a typical middle-class Argentine youth.' He also noticed that Che had lost his Argentine accent and he ridiculed him as a 'rejuvenated caricature of Cantinflas,' who was a renowned Mexican comedy actor.

Che assured Massetti that Castro was not a Communist.

'If he was we would at least have more arms,' said Guevara. 'Politically Fidel and his movement can be said to be 'revolutionary nationalist.' Of course it is anti-Yankee, in the measure that the Yankees are anti-revolutionaries. But in reality we don't preach anti-Yankeeism. We are against the United States because the United States is against our peoples. The person most attacked with the label of Communism is myself.'

Nevertheless Bigart warned the US embassy in Havana of Che's 'rather strong anti-US sentiment.' Che also had a vision of uniting the Americas:

'I consider my fatherland to be not only Argentina, but all of America,' he said. 'I have predecessors as glorious as [Cuban independence leader José] Martí and it is precisely in his land where I am adhering to his doctrine. What is more I cannot conceive that it can be called interference to give myself personally, to give myself completely, to offer my blood for a cause I consider just and popular, to help a people liberate themselves from tyranny… No country until now has denounced the American interference in Cuban affairs nor has a single daily newspaper accused the Yankees of helping Batista massacre his people. But many are concerned about me. I am a meddling foreigner who helps the rebels with his flesh and blood. Those who provide the arms for a civil war aren't meddlers. I am.'

However Che was respected for sharing the privations of his men, though he was still reading voraciously. However, he was not completely ascetic. According to a comrade: 'In Las Vega de Jiboca, Che met a black or rather mulatto girl with a very lovely body, called Zoila. Many women were crazy about him, and in that sense he was always very strict and respectful, but he liked that girl. They met and were together for some time.'

Eighteen-year-old single mother Zoila Rodríguez Garcia was corralling the cows when Che rode up on a mule, wearing 'a strange green uniform with a black beret.' He was looking for her father as the mule needed shoeing and Zoila volunteered.

'As I shoed the mule, I looked at him sideways and realized that he was watching me,' she said. 'But he was looking at me the way boys look at girls and I got really nervous... He kept looking at me in that way, with a stare that was a little bit naughtily.'

Later, over coffee, he asked here how she had learnt to shoe mules, then whether she was married or single. When her father came home, he told her that Guevara was an amazing man who had come to lift the Cuban people from their poverty and misery. She began running errands for the rebels, seeing Che occasionally. Later he asked her to stay with him and she worked in the kitchen and the hospital.

'I cannot deny it,' she said. 'As a woman I liked him a lot, especially his stare. He had such beautiful eyes, such a smile so calm that he could touch any heart, move any woman... He wanted to know all about the animals and the birds of the bush. He awoke in me a great and beautiful love, and I committed myself to him, not only as a combatant, but as a woman.'

With the anti-Batista coalition now badly fractured, the Communists of the Partido Socialista Popular now swung behind Castro. Members joined Che's Fourth Column in the Sierra Maestra, though they were warned to secrecy about their PSP membership. However, behind his back, there was speculation among Che's men about whether he was a *ñangaro*—a Red. Some pointed out that Che often quoted Lenin and compared him to José Martí and other Cuban nationalists. He mixed Cuban history and Marxism in his daily study session and when he taught the illiterate among his followers to read, Lenin's biography became a standard text.

Only Zoila did not receive the benefit of a political education. One day, when she saw one of his books, she was amazed to see it had golden letters. 'I asked him if they were made of gold,' she said. 'He thought the question was funny. He laughed and said: "That book is about Communism." I was too shy to ask him what Communism meant, because I had never heard the word before.'

'For Che, the guerrilla war wasn't just a military proving ground,' said one recruit, 'but also a cultural and educational one. He was concerned with forming the cadres of the revolution.'

Che believed that the Cuban revolution would naturally evolve towards Socialism.

'The guerrillas and the peasantry began to merge into a single mass,' he wrote later, 'without our being able to say at what precise moment on the long revolutionary road this happened, or at which moment the words became profoundly real, we were becoming part of the peasantry.'

And he was eager to have PSP members among their ranks, saying 'in the Sierra the only people who should be expelled are US journalists. If we persecute Communists, we will be doing up here what Batista is doing down there.'

Meanwhile Castro was making overtures to Batista. He sent a messenger saying that if the army was withdrawn from Oriente, he would agree to internationally supervised elections. Batista's rejection of this proposal was so impassioned that the messenger fled into exile. Meanwhile Castro was telling *Paris Match*, the *Chicago Tribune*, and anyone else who would listen that he was for free enterprise and foreign investment, and against nationalization. And in an article he wrote himself for the *Coronet*, he promised a provisional government full of middle-class professionals.

However, a letter revealing Che's distinctly pro-Communist views fell into Batista's hands—the messenger only escaped execution because of the intervention of the CIA. The letter was broadcast by Castro's former brother-in-law, who hated him vehemently. However, the effect was blunted when the army took twenty-three political prisoners from Santiago jail out into the Sierra and massacred them, claiming that they had been killed in action.

Che—'the Sniper'—struck back in his 'Wild Shot' column in *El Cubano Libre*. Why were there no army casualties he asked? And why no prisoners? These men had been murdered and the government were lying about it. And if they were lying about that, they were lying about the rebels getting Communist backing too. Even the CIA were fooled. Although Guevara may be Marxist in this thinking, he was not a Communist and they dismissed him as 'an idealist adventurer.'

On February 16, 1958, Castro gave the orders to attack an army camp Pino del Agua in Oriente. Although Che's 'sputniks' and landmines proved ineffective, the guerrillas overran the pickets and were only stopped when the main force rallied. A column of army reinforcements was wiped out and Che begged Castro for another chance to overrun the camp. A second wave was repulsed and Che begged to be allowed to lead a third assault. Although he gave his permission, Castro warned Che not to do anything 'suicidal.'

'I seriously suggest that you be careful. I order you not to take on any combat role. Take charge of directing people, which is an indispensable task at this time,' he wrote. He knew that Che would not go ahead with the assault if he could not take part in the fighting himself.

Castro said of Guevara: 'In a way, he even violated the rules of combat—that is, the ideal norms, the most perfect methods—risking his life in battle because of that character, tenacity, and spirit of his... So we had to lay down certain rules and guidelines for him to follow.'

He was right and Che withdrew. But it was the last time that Castro held Che back for his own safety.

A week after the attack on the army camp, Che's fellow countryman, Argentine racing driver Juan Manual Fangio, was kidnapped in Havana by the 26th of July movement. Released unharmed, he described his kidnappers as 'warm and friendly.' Castro further consolidated his position by drawing up legislation that introduced agrarian reform in his *territorio libre*. Cattle rustled from landowners were given to the peasants, which proved a popular move among the *guajiros*. Then in March, he set up a military training school at Minas del Frío, with Che as its titular head, though a former army lieutenant who had defected to the rebels actually ran it.

By this time the 'international' or 'Argentine Communist' 'Che' Guevara was a regular figure in the *anti-fidelísta* press. He was the most feared guerrilla leader in the Sierra Maestra. The army propaganda against him was particularly vehement. It was said that he was 'a murderer for hire, a pathological criminal... a mercenary who lent his services to international Communism, that he used terrorist methods and brainwashed women and took away their sons… any soldiers he took prisoner he tied to a tree and opened up their guts with a bayonet.'

In March 1958, the Catholic Church called for an end to the fighting and the formation of a government of national unity. Castro rejected this as pro-Batista, but just as he was about to be seen as an impediment to peace two of Batista's henchmen were indicted for murder. Batista threw out the indictment and the judge fled. Then he suspended the constitution and postponed the elections that were planned for June. The US reacted by banning any further arms shipments to Cuba. Batista obtained more weapons from Costa Rica and the Dominican Republic and on 12 March Castro and the 26th of July movement declared 'total war' on the regime.

No taxes were to be paid. Recruits to the army would be considered criminals, while judges and government employees should quit their jobs, or be considered traitors. And a general strike was called on April 9, which Castro hoped would be followed by a full-scale insurrection. But the whole thing fizzled out. The other opposition groups, excluding the Communists, continued working—as did the Batista-backed Confederación de Trabajadores Cubanos. The lesson learned by Castro and the Communists was simple: the only way to power was via armed struggle. At Che's suggestion, Castro stripped the leaders of the 26th of July movement of their powers and transferred them to the Sierra Maestro. Castro would now be in sole command of the opposition.

'The guerrilla conception emerged triumphant,' wrote Che. 'Fidel's standing and authority were consolidated… There now arose only one authoritative leadership, the Sierra, and concretely one single leader, one commander in chief, Fidel Castro.'

Others in the 26th of July movement condemned this gathering of power into a single pair of hands as *caudillismo*—'leaderism'. For Che, a committed Stalinist, it was no problem. However, he did find it strange that Fidel still did not make a formal pact with the PSP.

Realizing that the army were now preparing for a full-scale attack, Castro ordered his rebel army to withdraw to the northeast where Che commandeered a landowner's house at La Otila. He now devoted himself to training the new recruits who were flocking to join them. They were formed into a new column, No. 8.

As Batista's army encircled the guerrillas, they were getting low on weapons with not much more than two hundred functioning rifles to defend their remaining territory. Castro had little faith in their ability to hold out and planned to poison the water supplies if they were overrun. Meanwhile Che rushed from place to place, supervising the defenses as the army moved in. One new recruit accompanied him on a drive along a dirt-track road that skirted a precipice at break-neck speed in a jeep. At the end of the ride, Che confided in his terrified passenger that it was the first time he had driven—which was true. Until then, his driving experience had been confined to a motorbike.

As he went, Che pushed forward Castro's 'agrarian reforms' and 'taxed' recalcitrant plantation owners.

'Later, when our strength was sold,' wrote Che, 'we got even.'

In these endeavors, Che's right-hand man was a woman in her forties named Lidia, who had come to the Sierra Maestra when her only son had joined the rebels. Despite her courage and revolutionary zeal, Che eventually had to send her away as Cuban men were not used to taking orders from a woman. Later, when she was betrayed and murdered, he wrote: 'For me personally, Lidia occupies a special place. That is why I offer today these reminiscences to her—a modest flower laid on the mass grave that this once happy island became.'

The situation grew more desperate as the Nicaraguan dictator Anastasio Somoza García sent Batista thirty tanks and the US Department of Defense, despite the State Department's embargo, supplied the Cuban air force three hundred rockets from their stockpile in Guantánamo Bay. When Castro saw these rockets used against civilian targets, he swore that he would make the Americans pay.

'When this war ends, I'll start a much longer and bigger war of my own: the war I am going to fight against them,' he wrote. 'I realize that will be my true destiny.'

However, in radio interviews Castro still denied being a Communist and that, after the revolution, the 26th of July movement would become a political party which would 'fight with the arms of the Constitution and the law.' Meanwhile he continued his attempts to win over the army, writing a flattering note to General Eulogio Cantillo, head of Batista's forces in Oriente, and warning via the press that 'every entrance to the Sierra Maestro is like the pass at Thermopylae.'

Che also played the game. While he gave assurances to the American estate managers he came into contact with, he told his comrades: 'In the end we will have to fight them. I would die with a smile on my lips, on the crest of a hill, behind a rock, fighting against these people.'

While Castro called a meeting of 350 peasants to discuss how to harvest the coffee and proposed introducing a Sierra currency, Che busied himself preparing the defenses as now the whole of Batista's army began closing in. Things were not looking good for the rebels. Facing air attack from planes carrying rockets and machineguns, guerrillas began to desert, but Che, as always, meted out stern discipline. Eventually even Che was affected by their reverses. On July 3, he noted: 'A little combat broke out in which we retreated very quickly. The position was bad and they were encircling us, but we put up little resistance. Personally I noted something I had never felt before: the need to live. That had better be corrected at the next opportunity.' Others who demonstrated this 'need to live' were given instead a summary execution.

On the eve of battle, Che used the guerrilla's new radio link to speak to his mother. She wished him a happy 30th birthday. She also wrote to him giving him news of his family. By this time he rarely wrote to his parents or his wife and daughter, though he had the opportunity to do so. Even his diaries are stripped of any personal detail.

General Cantillo's plan was to encircle Castro's guerrilla army, then tighten the noose. But the terrain of the Sierra Maestra, which its thick jungle and deep ravines, made this impossible. As the guerrillas fell back, advancing army units found that they were cut off, allowing the guerrillas to go on the offensive.

During the counter-attack Raúl Castro seized American sailors and marines from a bus on the outskirts of Guantánamo Bay Navy Base, along with American and Canadian employees of the United Fruit Company and US-owned mining concerns, claiming that he had taken the hostages in protest at the base's support of Batista's forces. Even Che thought he had gone too far and complained of Raúl's 'extremism.'

In retaliation, napalm from Guantánamo Bay was used against Che's forces defending Mompié. Castro ordered Raúl to release the hostages unharmed and made a public statement that hostage-taking was not rebel policy.

However, Raúl did not release the hostages immediately. But, as if to demonstrate the US administration's power over Batista, the air strikes ceased. Raúl used the lull to resupply. Then, when he released the hostages on 18 July, the air strikes resumed.

Che's forces only managed to hold the line against the army's onslaught. There was an air strike against the hospital at Mompié and Che lamented the deaths of several 'most loved collaborators and true revolutionaries.' However, Castro had surrounded an army camp at El Jigüe. The commander there, Major José Quevedo, had been Castro's classmate at law school and Castro wrote to him offering, 'an honorable and dignified surrender.'

'We are not at war with the army, we are at war with tyranny,' wrote Castro. His men would be treated well and his officers would be permitted to keep their weapons. 'It will not be a surrender to an enemy of the fatherland, but to a sincere revolutionary, to a fighter who struggles for the good of all Cubans.'

When Major Quevedo refused, Castro got one of his men, pretending to be an army wireless operator, to radio the air force, telling them that the camp had fallen. This brought in an air strike. Quevedo then surrendered. Castro took a huge haul of guns and ammunition, and over 288 prisoners. Some of the officers, including Quevedo, then changed sides. But the bulk of the prisoner were handed back in a two-day truce organized by the Red Cross later that week.

Che used the truce to move up his men. He surrounded the army camp at Las Vegas. Emissaries were sent out, who offered to leave behind their food if they were allowed to withdraw with their weapons. Che rejected this, only to find, a little time later, that the column was withdrawing, flying a white flag, and a Red Cross flag. Che ordered his men to open fire and led the pursuit himself. Resistance quickly collapsed and Che advanced so quickly that his men came under friendly fire.

'I had the uncomfortable situation of being besieged by our own forces, who opened fire every time they saw a helmet,' he wrote.

In this action, Che captured a tank, which was stuck in the mud. The air force tried to bomb it while the guerrilla tried to pull it free. A week later the team of oxen freed it, but broke its steering wheel in the process, rendering it useless.

Elsewhere in the line, there had been setbacks. A second army retreat had been a ruse and in the counter-attack, René Ramos Latour, one of the leading anti-Communist guerrillas, was killed.

'We were political enemies,' Che wrote that evening, 'but he knew how to die fulfilling his duty on the front line. Whoever dies like that does so because he feels an internal impulse that I denied him and that I will now rectify.'

Two weeks later, one of Che's closest comrades, Beto Pesant, was killed when an anti-aircraft shell exploded. Che was badly shaken.

'When I heard the explosion, I saw that Guevara's mule, Armando, was injured and had thrown him into the air,' said Zoila Rodríguez. 'I ran to his side, but he was already getting up. I looked over at Pesant and saw that he was missing an arm. His head was destroyed and his chest was open… I began to scream: "Beto, don't die, don't die!" They attended to him quickly. The *comandante* told me: "Zoila, he's dead."' Later, at the funeral, 'we all cried and when I looked at Guevara he had tears in his eyes.'

On August 7, 1958, the army began to pull out of its last stronghold in the Sierra Maestra. Another truce was organized for the exchange of prisoners. This time Che and Fidel met with army officers for coffee. They even took a ride on a helicopter and, in a rare act of kindness in this divisive war, the army airlifted in some blood plasma for the rebels.

An army officer, who Che believed talked for the regime, proposed that they reach a peaceful solution by forming a new provisional government under the senior justice of the Supreme Court. But Castro was not interested. He still believed that he could convince General Cantillo to come over to his side and he now began entering into talks with the Communists who, several weeks later, sent a permanent representative to the Sierra. Meanwhile Che busied himself with dispensing revolutionary justice, noting that he had executed an army deserter who had attempted to rape a girl.

Although the army's offensive in the Sierra Maestra had been soundly defeated, when the truce ended, the air force resumed bombing and strafing. Castro's plan was to widen the war. Raúl had already started a second front in the Sierra Cristal to the east. Che was to leave the Sierra and take the war to central and western Cuba. He was itching for action but found it difficult to put a volunteer force together. This was not helped by him telling recruits that they would go hungry, be in action almost all the time, and only half of them would come back. Zoila volunteered to go with him, but he refused to take her. She was to stay behind with his mule, which she 'cared for as if he were a real Christian.'

Despite incessant bombing, Che assembled a force of 148 men with six jeeps and pick-ups to transport them. But two days before they were to leave, the army seized two pickups loaded with ammunition freshly arrived from Miami and all the petrol they needed for the trip. Che resolved to go on foot.

In forty-six days, they marched nearly three hundred miles heavily laden with ammunition and carrying a forty-rocket bazooka through a cyclone that made the roads impassable. They had to ford swollen rivers and cross hostile territory that was swarming with informers. They had little food, were plagued with mosquitoes, and suffered a painful foot condition the peasants called *mazamorra*. Along the way they were ambushed by the army, loosing many men. The only break they got was that, on September 20, General Francisco Tabernilla Dolz, Batista's chief of staff, announced that the 'invading' force led by Che Guevara had been destroyed.

Along the way Che said he 'attempted to clean the scum out of the column.' On October 7, he cashiered seven men. The following night Herman Marks, a former convict from Milwaukee who had fought for the US in Korea, also left.

'He was wounded and ill, but fundamentally did not fit the troop,' said Guevara.

Though he had risen to the rank of captain, was an excellent trainer of men and recklessly brave in combat, Marks was disruptive in camp and rather too eager to act as Che's executioner.

Those who remained formed a tight-knit unit due to Che's stern discipline and the privations they had shared. Even for minor infractions, Che would threaten a man with death, then deprive him of rations for five days 'so they would know what real hunger was.' But as a leader he was respected. A foreigner and an intellectual, he read books they could not understand, but he took the same risks as them and demanded no privileges as an officer. And he had sacrificed more than they had. He had left the beautiful Zoila behind.

On October 16, 1958, they arrived in the safety of the Sierra Escambray in the Sancti-Spíritus Mountains to the north of the city of Trinidad. In the area there were a number of competing opposition factions that could easily betray him for their own advantage. Now far from the control of Castro, Che threw in his lot with the Communists of the PSP and the Revolutionary Student Directorate, though he had been told not to. Their representatives had heard of his awesome reputation that had been built up by government propaganda and they were impressed. And Che had now assumed the image that comes down to us over the years. During the march, he had lost the battered cap he had inherited from Ciro Redondo, a *Granma* veteran who had been killed in a firefight in the Sierra Maestra. This upset him immensely, but he now adopted the black beret which would become his trademark.

Enrique Oltuski, the local representative of the 26th of July movement, caught up with Che one night at his camp.

'I had this image of Che that I had seen published in the newspapers,' he said. 'None of these faces was that face. But there was a man, of regular build, who was wearing a beret over very long hair. The beard was not very thick. He was dressed in a black cape with his shirt open.

115

The flames of the bonfire and the moustache, which fell over either side of the mouth, gave him a Chinese aspect. I thought of Genghis Khan.'

Oltuski and Che soon fell out when Che asked Oltuski for details of all the banks in the area so he could stick them up. They also disagreed over land reform. Che boiled over with indignation when Oltuski suggested that land should be sold to the peasants at cost and easy credit terms.

'What a reactionary idea!' yelled Che, who favored free distribution of the land. 'How can we charge those who work the land?'

Oltuski pointed out that if they simply gave land to the peasants they would ruin it as they had done in Mexico. Also they could not adopt such openly Communist policies with the US looking on.

'So you are one of those who believes we can make a revolution behind the backs of the Americans,' said Guevara. 'What a shitface you are! The revolution must be a life-and-death struggle against imperialism from the outset. A true revolution cannot be disguised.'

Soon PSP members would be attached to his column. The leadership showed their gratitude by sending a copy of Mao Tse-tung's *On Guerrilla Warfare* and cans of Argentine maté. Castro wrote, warning him about cosying up to the Communists again. However, Che himself was not an unalloyed fan of the PSP.

'The PSP had not seen clearly enough the role of guerrilla warfare,' said Che, 'or the personal role of Fidel in our revolutionary struggle.'

Nor did he have much respect for the Communists' ability to fight.

'The Communists are able to train cadres who will let themselves be ripped to shreds in a dark dungeon without a word,' he said, 'but no cadres who will take a machine-gun nest by assault.

On the other hand, there were far more dangerous 'allies' in the Sierra Escambray. The local warlord Comandante Jesús Carreras warned Che not to pass through his territory. When Che went to confront him, he found Carreras 'had already drunk half a bottle of liquor, which approximated half his daily quota.' And Carreras quickly backed down. His warning had been intended for other opposition groups, he said. But after the revolution, he returned to the Sierra Escambray and, in 1961, was hunted down and executed.

Che ordered the burning of all the voting centres in the area to hamper the forthcoming elections, then led an attack on the garrison at Güinía de Miranda. He was warned not do to this by one guerrilla leader, as it lay within his patch. Che took no notice. He was hindered by another group who stole forty pairs of new boots badly needed by his men and he had to demote another guerrilla leader who claimed he had met Castro, when he hadn't.

The other guerrilla leaders would not support Guevara's attack on Güinía de Miranda. But Che went head anyway. When four shots from the bazooka missed the barracks—resulting in a withering firefight— Che grabbed the bazooka himself, hit the barracks and the fourteen soldiers insides surrendered immediately. All-in-all the raid was a waste of time as they only collected eight rifles and a little ammunition, for a heavy outlay. However, Che stole a jeep which he left as a present for a guerrilla leader who had refused to participate.

Due to the continued non-cooperation of other guerrilla groups and the failure of his own men, Che failed to make a headline-grabbing attack on election day, November 3. However, another group of *fidelístas* under his old comrade Camilio Cienfuegos to the north had brought traffic in the region to a standstill. As expected Batista's chosen successor, the former prime minister Andrés Rivero Agüero won due to massive voter fraud. By this time, few people thought that their future lay in the hands of the politicians in Havana, but rather the *barbudos*—the 'bearded ones'—in the Sierras, who were now determined to prevent Rivero Agüero's inauguration ever taking place.

At Cabellete de Casas, Che set up a new rearguard base with fortifications, a system of trenches, radio communication, a military school, an armory, a hospital, and an all-important tobacco factory. He also started a new newspaper call *El Miliciano*—'The Militiaman'. At the new base, which he named Ñico López after his fallen comrade, he recruited the recruited three vital disciples for the post-war struggle. They were the twenty-one-year-old accountancy student Orlando Borrego, who became treasurer— though Che forced him to take a military training course; Jesús Suárez Gayol—*El Rudio* ('The Blonde')—a daredevil whose exploits include rushing into a police station with a stick of dynamite and a pistol, though he manage to set himself on fire during this assault; and the lawyer Miguel Ángel Duque de Estrada, who was employed as a judge to impose the guerrilla legal code on the area. He was told to suspend the use of firing squads as executions might discourage defections from the army. These three men were not Marxists to start with, but Che talked them around to his political philosophy.

Che supported his efforts by imposing 'war taxes' on local enterprises. Other guerrilla groups who did the same were forced to stop and the money they had raised was confiscated. He also tried to ban alcohol and the lottery, but villagers revolted and he was forced to back down. He even tried to regulate the sexual morality of his youthful troops. This, again, proved impossible, especially when Che himself took a new lover. He name was Aleida March and, according to a comrade, 'she was one of the most beautiful women in Cuba and her preference for Che could not but provoke some resentment against that damned Argentine who carried her off as a war trophy.'

However, Batista's secret police identified her as *Teta Mancheda*— 'Stained Tit'—because of a birthmark that spread from her breast to the collar bone—or *Cara Cortada*—'Scarface'—because of marks on her cheek from a dogbite when she was young.

The twenty-four-year-old Aleida had a lower-middle class Spanish background—Cuba was still racially segregated at the time. She was a blonde. At university she had joined the 26th of July movement and she had been sent from Santa Clara to take cash to the guerrillas. Naturally, she had already heard of the legendary fighter Che Guevara, but in the flesh she was unimpressed, characterizing him as 'old… skinny and dirty'.

Aleida had something of a reputation of her own. She would smuggle weapons and bombs under her 1950s full-length shirt.

'She wasn't afraid of anything,' recalled a friend. 'She was totally dedicated, very serious, single and wasn't one for parties and that sort of thing.'

During one trip, she heard that her cover had been blown. There was no way she could return to Santa Clara and she asked Che's permission to stay at Cabellete de Casas. Che was against the idea. He usually did not allow women to stay in the guerrilla camps, but in this case he had no choice. Aleida was anti-Communist, so there was friction between the two of them.

'She was difficult to get on with,' said a friend of Che's. But soon she fell in love with him. The affair was fraught: '…she was terribly jealous of everyone and everything that had been close to Che before she knew him.'

Che had little time for love. His bases were being bombarded daily by the air force and, in late November, the army moved up three heavily armed columns, led by tanks. In a six-day battle, the guerrillas halted the advance, even capturing a tank. Guevara then set about blowing up the road and railway bridges, cutting Havana off from the east of the island.

He was in combat constantly and took unnecessary risks, but his only injuries were a cut above the eyebrow and a fractured elbow sustained when he fell off a roof. The arm was splinted and set in a cast, and he continued to fight.

One night Aleida was unable to sleep and, around three or four in the morning, left her room and went out to sit by the road. Che raced up in a jeep and asked her what she was doing there. When she replied that she could not sleep, he said: 'I am going to attack Cabaiguán. Do you want to come along?'

She said, 'Sure', and jumped in beside him. 'And from that moment on, I never left his side—or let him out of my sight.'

His doctor Dr Oscar Fernández Mell, noted: 'Suddenly Aleida was with Che wherever he went, in combat, everywhere… She carried his papers and washed his clothes.'

Some were not so observant. Che's general staff orderly Alberto Castellanos fancied himself as a ladies' man and tried to chat her up.

Che was there at the time and made it very clear that Aleida was not available.

'From the way Che looked at me, I said to myself: "Beat it, Alberto, there's nothing for you here."'

It was an intensely sexual affair. Much later, during a trip to India, Che's roommate read one of the letters Che was writing to Aleida, who was then his wife. It was 'absolutely pornographic,' he said.

Word quickly spread that Guevara was traveling with 'three women: a blonde'—Aleida—'a black, and a jabao'—the Cuban word for a light-skinned mulatto. The latter two were his bodyguards, Harry Villegas and Jesús Parra, or 'Parrita'. They were beardless teenagers, whose long hair made it easy for them to be mistaken for girls. In fact with Che the disciplinarian and Aleida, who was strict and middle class, they formed a revolutionary family.

On December 22, 1958, Che wrote to Castro telling him that the key town of Fomento had fallen and he had taken 141 prisoners along with 139 shotguns, 98 Springfields, twenty-one Garands, one .20-calibre machine-gun, one Thompson machine-gun, one 81mm mortar, two radio cars, three jeeps and two trucks—one of them armored—plus fifteen grenades and a large amount of ammunition.

'After our forces withdrew, the enemy planes carried out a merciless bombardment against the civilian population of the city, killing two children and wounding several civilians,' he continued.

Soon after the towns of Cabairguán, Placetas, Caibarién, and Remedios fell. More armaments were captured and Batista's soldiers were surrendering even when they had the military advantage, sensing that the civilian population had turned against them. Now only the garrison at Camajuaní lay between the rebels and Santa Clara, the fourth largest city in Cuba.

With a number of towns in rebel hands it was becoming increasingly difficult for Che to keep order. He put a ban on his men visiting the bars and brothels in the towns they had taken, but his men had suffered months of abstinence in the bush. A grateful brothel-owner sent out a case of rum and a truck load of prostitutes. Platoon leader Enrique Acevedo found the ambush he was organizing melting away as his men disappeared into the bush with the girls and he had to call the brothel owner and ask him to take the girls back.

On December 26, 1958, Castro, who was besieging the garrison at Moffo, wrote by flashlight to Che saying: 'The war is won. The enemy is collapsing with a resounding crash. We have 10,000 men bottled up in Oriente. Those in Camagüey'—to Che's rear—'have no way of escaping.'

Castro's major concern now was that 'the advance towards Matanzas and Havana be carried out exclusively by the 26th of July forces... to take over Havana when the dictatorship falls, if we don't want the weapons from Camp Columbia'—the military headquarters there— 'distributed among all the various groups, which would present a very serious problem in the future.'

Castro's efforts to try to co-opt the army were now paying off and negotiations between them began in earnest. Meanwhile both Castro and Batista knew that the battle for Santa Clara would be crucial. At the geographic centre of the island, it controlled all the major communication routes. As a city of 150,000, it was defended by a garrison of 2,500 with ten tanks. A further 1,000 reinforcements were on their way from Havana on an armored train, loaded with arms, ammunition, and communications equipment.

On December 28, Guevara attacked with a force of 340 men—largely exhausted, undernourished and inexperienced—to take on a force ten times bigger. When they reached the university, one of the rebels asked how many of Batista's men they were facing. About five thousand he was told.

'Good,' he said. 'With our *jefe* that is no problem.'

After establishing a headquarters in the university, they took the radio station, where Che broadcast to the city asking for civilians to barricade the streets, build Molotov cocktails, and stockpile provisions. Batista's forces responded by bombing the guerrillas' positions and the city itself. That night, with the help of civilians, Che's men infiltrated the city centre.

Within his own force Guevara continued to maintain exacting standards. He reprimanded one of his men who he had disarmed because he had accidentally let his gun go off, telling him with his customary dryness: 'Go up to the front line barehanded and get yourself another gun... if you are man enough.'

Later when he went to visit his wounded in the hospital, a dying man touched his arm and said: 'Remember me, *comandante*? You sent me to get a gun at Remedios... I brought it here.'

He died a few minutes later.

'It seemed to me that he was pleased to have proved his courage,' said Guevara. 'Such was our Rebel Army.'

Guerrillas had already cut the Matanzas-Santa Clara road preventing reinforcements getting through, so Guevara concentrated his attention on the armored train. It had been forced out of the city centre by Roberto '*El Vaquerito*' (little cowboy) Rodríguez's *Escuadra Suicída*—'Suicide Squad'—and retreated at speed.

'The Suicide Squad was an example of revolutionary morale and only selected volunteers joined it,' said Guevara. 'But whenever a man died—and it happened in every battle—when the new candidate was named, those not chosen would be grief-stricken and even cry. How curious to see those seasoned and noble warriors showing their youth by their tears of despair, because they did not have the honor of being in the front line of combat and death.'

Che taunted that Batista's men were prepared to fight only at long range, from comfortable positions, against a virtually unarmed enemy— 'in the true style of colonizers versus the Indians of the North American West,' said Guevara. However, the rebels had taken the precaution of blowing up the rails. The train crashed and the guerrillas moved in with Molotov cocktails.

It is unclear what happened next. Guevara said: 'The train—thanks to its armor plate—became a veritable oven for its soldiers. After several hours, the entire crew surrendered.' And the heroic attack on the armored train is still commemorated in Cuba. However, Eloy Gutiérrez Menoyo, the leader of another guerrilla group who was there, said a deal was done. He claimed that he had opened the negotiations, but Guevara had outbid him. Batista said that the train's commander 'deserted after receiving $350,000 or $1 million from Che Guevara.' Gutiérrez Menoyo said that he asked Che on several occasions what he had given for the train.

'He only laughed and never confessed the truth to me,' said Menoyo. 'If they had surrendered the train to me, there was an incredible amount of supplies there and that would have allowed us to launch the final offensive. Che never gave me a specific answer.'

Either way Guevara's men took four hundred prisoners, along with six bazookas, six hundred automatic rifles, fourteen machine-guns, five 60mm mortars, one 20mm cannon and one million rounds of ammunition. It was the largest weapons haul of the war.

During the action, Che seems to have lost something—his heart. Aleida had dashed across the street under fire. Later, he confessed that every moment she had been out of sight had been agony. He was in love with her. And once the battle was over, he posed her in front of the derailed train.

'Aleida,' he said, 'I am going to take a picture of you for history.'

It was their Bonnie and Clyde moment.

The loss of the armored train had a devastating effect on the morale of Batista's soldiers. On December 30, the garrison of Los Caballitos surrendered. Soldiers barricaded in church also gave themselves up. The occupants of the police headquarters fought on. In the previous days, they had tortured and executed a number of civilians for treason or, sometimes, minor crimes, and feared reprisals. But the headquarters were soon overrun. However, there were still 1,300 in the city's main garrison and army snipers on the tenth floor of the Gran Hotel.

To the south the city of Trinidad had fallen. Castro had taken Moffo after a ten-day siege and was now moving on Santiago de Cuba, the island's second city. He met General Cantillo, who agreed to fly to Havana, organize a military coup, and arrest Batista. Instead, at a New

Year's Eve party at Camp Columbia, Cantillo warned Batista of the coup. Batista handed over power to Carlos Manuel Piedra, the senior Supreme Court Justice, who named Cantillo as armed forces chief, headquarters at Camp Columbia outside Havana, and leader of the new ruling junta. Meanwhile Batista and his family, along with president-elect Rivero Agüero and a number of Batista's most notorious henchmen headed for the nearby military airstrip. And in the early hours of January 1, 1959, they flew to safety in the Dominican Republic. American mobster Meyer Lansky also fled Cuba that day.

*

Meyer Lansky (1902–83)

Born Meyer Suchowljansky in Belorussia, he arrived in New York City as an immigrant at the age of nine. While a teenager on the Lower East Side, he became friends with Charles 'Lucky' Luciano and Benjamin 'Bugsy' Siegel. During Prohibition, he became a bootlegger and in the 1930s moved into the casino business. During World War II, Lansky, a Jew, helped recruit Luciano in Operation Underworld, where gangsters used their muscle to prevent sabotage in the docks and their influence in Sicily to aid the Allied invasion there.

After the war, Lansky took a stake in Siegel's Las Vegas casino, the Flamingo, continuing to invest after Siegel was murdered in 1947 when the casino failed to make money. However, most of Lansky's gambling operations were in Florida and Saratoga Springs, New York, and he increasingly moved off shore to Cuba to run the mob's gambling interests there. In 1953, Lansky was convicted for conspiracy and gambling, and his casinos in the US were closed. For the rest of his life, he was under investigation by the Internal Revenue Service, the Immigration Service, and, later, the FBI.

When Fidel Castro came to power in 1959, he closed Lansky's Riviera casino in Cuba. Lansky had already fled. In the early 1960s, Lansky organized a profit-skimming ring in Las Vegas, but later sold his casino interests in the US to build up his business in the Bahamas. In 1970, to escape indictment, Lansky fled to Israel, claiming citizenship under Israel's 'Law of Return' that welcomes any Jew returning to the traditional Jewish homeland. Lansky figured that he could go on running his crime syndicate from Tel Aviv. Like other fugitive Jewish-American gangsters he had taken the precaution of funneling millions of dollars into Israeli government bonds, charitable organizations, and Israeli businesses.

When his biography *Lansky* came out, it alleged that Lansky had advanced knowledge of the indictment and had been warned to get out of the US. An Israeli newspaper serialized the book and the press demanded that Lansky be expelled. His application for Israeli citizenship was denied in 1972 and, in a much publicized flight, he sought sanctuary in Paraguay. When this was denied, he ended up back in the US where he faced several indictments. Over the next four years, he fought all the charges and won. He went into retirement in Miami Beach. But his legal bills, medical expenses for a persistent heart condition, and the care of a handicapped son left him impoverished. When he died in 1983, it was found that the trust fund he had left for his wife and son was worthless.

*

General Cantillo went on the radio, claiming that: 'What we have done here in [Camp] Columbia has the approval of Dr Fidel Castro.'

Within hours, Castro was on the air repudiating this and denouncing the junta. Later that day Cantillo was deposed by Colonel Ramón Barquín, who had been imprisoned after an earlier attempted coup against Batista.

When news reached Santa Clara that Batista had fled, the garrison opened negotiations, but Che said he would accept nothing less than unconditional surrender. Less than an hour later, the soldiers dropped their weapons and came out onto the street to be greeted by the cheering populous. In the meantime, the snipers in the Gran Hotel were dislodged and were executed after a summary hearing two hours later. Four of them were policemen. The other five were considered *chivatos*— informers. Revolutionary justice was meted out to many others including the police chief Colonel Cornelio Rojas who, at the last moment, asked to be allowed to give the order to fire. It was granted.

The notorious butcher Colonel Joaquín Casilla, who was reputed to keep a collection of the ears of his victims, was caught fleeing the city wearing a straw hat and a 26th of July armband. He tried to persuade his captors to come with him and join the new military junta. When he was told that he was going to be taken to see Che, he blanched and asked if there was not some other *jefe* he could see.

When Che met him, he greeted him with the words: 'So you the murderer of Jesús Menéndez'—the Communist sugar-union leader. Later it was announced that Casillas had been shot dead trying to escape while on his way to see Che.

Santiago de Cuba surrendered and Castro sent orders for Che to move on Havana where he was to occupy La Cabaña, the old fortress that overlooks the mouth of the harbor. Camilo Cienfuegos went ahead to take Camp Columbia, while Che did a little mopping up—which included the summary execution of more *chivatos* and a speech thanking the people of Santa Clara for their help in the cause of revolution. And at 3 pm, Che headed for Havana with Aleida at his side. The crucial battle for Santa Clara had cost the lives of just six guerrillas and less than three hundred of Batista's men had died.

Chapter Seven—Our Man in Havana, 1959-1964

Cheering crowds greeted the young, dynamic, fun-loving, *Cubano* Camilo Cienfuegos when he entered Havana on the morning of January 3, 1959. Hardly anyone noticed when bedraggled Argentine Che Guevara arrived at dawn the following day with Aleida and some of his closest aids. He was tired, dirty, dressed in rags, and relegated to taking an objective that was outside the city proper.

The three thousand troops stationed in the Spanish colonial fortress of La Cabaña had already surrendered to 26th of July militiamen. Che referred to the militiamen as a 'neocolonial army.' While they could teach the guerrillas how to march, the rebels could teach them how to fight. He and Aleida then installed themselves in the comandante's house, overlooking Havana.

Che had been deliberately steered out of the limelight because he was a Communist. Camilo, on the other hand, wore a Stetson and played baseball. His image would play better in Washington. Meanwhile Castro had taken Santiago, which he had proclaimed the provisional capital of Cuba and Manual Urrutia flew in from Venezuela to be president. A liberal politician, he had been the tribunal president at Castro's trial after the 26th July insurrection and argued that because of the "abnormal situation" in Cuba he had been within his constitutional rights to take up arms, but was outvoted. Che was given a more clandestine role to perform. He was to be Fidel's willing executioner.

After years in the Sierras, the opportunities offered by Havana's nightlife—particularly its notorious sex trade—was too much for the rebels to resist and young men with beards were very much in demand by beautiful women. To maintain some discipline and with an eye to the image of the rebel army, Che staged a mass wedding between his men and the lovers they had picked up along the way—there had already been a decree in the Sierras obliging guerrilla fighters to marry the women they had impregnated. Soon even male models in advertisements sported the obligatory beard.

As Castro began his triumphal procession across the island, there were other problems to sort out in Havana. The bearded rebel army bivouacked in the hotel lobbies. Meanwhile crowds attacked casinos, parking meters, and other symbols of Batista's corrupt regime. Diehard *batístianos* turned to sniping. Others sought refuge in foreign embassies, while there were manhunts to track down corrupt politicians, secret policemen and other agents of the old regime. However, some semblance of order was soon imposed by the 26th of July militiamen.

Camilo Cienfuegos had installed himself in Camp Columbia. Surrounded by heel-clicking military men, he received the American ambassador unshod, with his feet on the table. Meanwhile the Revolutionary Student Directory had taken over the presidential palace. Camilo suggested that a couple of cannon balls would clear them out. Che said that they should not waste the cannon balls. He went to the presidential palace and straightened things out. When Castro arrived in Havana on January 8, Urrutia had been installed in the presidential palace.

The entire population of Havana turned out to greet Castro, who rode into town on a captured tank with Che beside him. Castro also jumped aboard *Granma*, which had been brought into Havana harbor. With him at his later public appearances were Camilo and Raúl. Che was kept discretely out of sight in La Cabaña, while the politics were being dealt with.

With a dove of peace direct from a Cuban *santería* on one shoulder and Camilo's beard on the other, Castro made his victory speech.

'The Revolution was won by the people and not by any *comandante*,' he said. 'How am I doing, Camilo?'

Castro himself moved into the Havana Hilton, which was later renamed the Havana *Libre*.

The Revolutionary Students Directory were persuaded to disarm, but the Communist leaders returned from exile. They started publishing their banned newspaper, *Hoy*, and called for mass demonstrations in support of the victorious rebels. The Washington and Caracas had already recognized the new regime and, on January 10, Moscow followed suit.

Guevara was not entirely overlooked though. Back in Buenos Aires, the exiled Cuban poet Nicolás Guillén, a Communist, wrote a poem comparing him to José de San Martín, the Argentine soldier and statesman who liberated Argentina, Chile, and Peru from Spanish rule. Che was already a legend.

Although Urrutia was president, Castro handpicked the government. The first shock was the appointment of Dr José Miró Cardona as prime minister. As a lawyer, he had represented American corporations and defended some of Cuba's most corrupt politicians and Batista's henchmen, including Joaquín Casillas when he stood trial for the murder of Jesús Menéndez. But he was pro-American. Harvard-educated Regino Boti, returned from the US, to become economics minister. Che's vocal opponent Erique Oltuski became minister of communications. And Castro himself was to be commander in chief of the armed forces.

Laws were quickly enacted banning prostitution and gambling. Che found that his men enjoyed cock-fighting, so he banned that too and brought in Communists to give them political education. This soon earned him the new title 'Chief of the Department of Training of the Revolutionary Armed Forces.'

The property of Batista and his henchmen would be confiscated and the ministries would be cleansed of corrupt officials. Political parties were to be banned and Castro would rule by 'direct democracy'—that is, by judging the reaction to proposals he made at mass rallies. However, Fidel had come to power through military might and he knew that his real power base lay in the army. But first it had to be purged. And Che was the man to do it.

While Colonel Barquín was made head of this military academy and other officers were sent off into 'gilded exile' as military attachés, summary trials began in La Cabaña where Guevara had set up a 'Cleansing Commission'—though the final decision lay with him as 'supreme prosecutor.'

On hand to administer revolutionary justice was Che's old comrade Herman Marks. Estimates of those killed range from two hundred to seven hundred—the official figure is 550. Raúl, now military governor of Oriente, shot more there—on one occasion machine-gunning seventy in front of a bulldozed trench. Che never had any doubt that these summary executions were entirely justified.

It was then, in a letter to Luis Paredes in Buenos Aires, he wrote: 'The executions by firing squads are not only a necessity for the people of Cuba, but also an imposition by the people.' he wrote. He put it rather more bluntly to an old colleague visiting from Mexico City: 'Look, in this thing either you kill first, or else you get killed.'

In the middle of January, Castro decided that some of the more high profile trials should take place in the sports stadium in Havana. The world, which had been sympathetic to the Cuban Revolution, was repulsed by the sight of crowds baying for blood, even though the culprits were torturers and multiple murderers. Why had the critics not spoken out when Batista was committing his atrocities? asked Castro. Washington was in no position to criticize after the US government had dropped the bomb on Hiroshima. And he warned that if the 'gringos' tried to invade Cuba it would cost them '200,000 dead Americans.' However, after his visit to Washington, Castro ordered that the executions were stopped. Che disagreed passionately, but obeyed.

'There were over a thousand prisoners of war with more arriving all the time, and many did not have dossiers,' said Miguel Ángel Duque de Estrada, head of the *Comisión de Depuración* or 'Cleansing Commission'. 'We did not even know all of their names. But we had a job to do, which was to cleanse the defeated army. Che always had a clear idea about the need to cleanse the army and exact justice on those found to be war criminals.'

Che's parents, sister, and brother arrived in Havana on January 9, on a plane the government had sent to collect Cuban exiles in Buenos Aires.

Two weeks later Hilda and three-year-old Hildita arrived from Lima, though the fearless guerrilla leader could not face meeting them at the airport. The whole family were worried about what Ernesto would do now. His father wanted him to return to medicine. Che said that, as they both had the same name, his father could substitute for him and 'begin killing people without risk.' For himself, Che knew he had a long way to go.

'I myself don't know where I will lay my bones to rest,' he said.

When Hilda eventually caught up with him, Guevara had some bad news to impart. His private life had moved on.

'With a candor that always characterized him, Ernesto forthrightly told me that he had another woman, who he had met in the campaign of Santa Clara,' she said. 'The pain was deep in me, but, following our convictions, we agreed on a divorce. I am still affected by the memory of the moment when, realizing my hurt, he said: "Better I had died in combat." For a moment I looked at him without saying anything. Though I was losing so much at the time, I thought of the fact that there were so many more important tasks to be done, for which he was so vital: he *had* to have remained alive. He had to build a new society. He had to work hard to help Cuba avoid the errors of Guatemala; he had to give his whole effort to the struggle for the liberation of America. No, I was happy that he had not died in combat, sincerely happy, and I tried to explain it to him this way, ending with: "Because of all this, I want you always." Moved, he said: "If that's how it is, then it's all right… friends, and comrades?"'

He took time off to walk hand in hand in La Cabaña with Hilda, even though the two of them had agreed to divorce and Aleida hated the sight of her. He also let Hildita play in his office and visited on her birthday. He moved his parents into the posh Hotel Comodoro in the western suburbs of Havana, where he would visit them by helicopter. He gave them a whirlwind tour of his old headquarters and the battlefields where he had been victorious—though when they traveled without him Che insisted that they pay for their own petrol and meals.

The whole family were on hand when, on February 2, the government conferred Cuban nationality 'by birth' on any foreigner who had spent two years fighting Batista. This had been enacted largely for Che's benefit.

On February 14, the family suddenly decided to return to Buenos Aires. Che turned up to see them off with Raúl Castro. At the airport an Argentine approached Guevara to shake his hand. Che obliged, then the man asked for an autograph. Che turned away, saying: 'I am not a movie star.'

In a last minute gesture, when the flight was called, his father slipped the gold watch off his wrist, which was an heirloom given to him by Che's beloved grandmother, and gave it to him. Che pulled off the watch of his own wrist and gave it to his father. It was the watch he had been given when he was promoted *comandante*. Later, Che donated the gold wristband from another watch he had been given to the Cuban national reserves.

The pressures of the executions and the family began to tell on Che. His asthma came back, this time accompanied by anemia and emphysema. He moved out of La Cabaña to a former batístiano's house at Tarará, ten miles east of Havana, and was told to limit himself to one cigar a day. One visitor recalled finding him smoking a cigar about a foot-and-a-half long.

'Don't worry about the doctor,' said Che with a mischievous smile. 'I am being good to my word: one cigar a day, and not one more.'

That the famously austere Che Guevara should be living it up in a luxurious seaside residence drew some criticism in the press. Che defended himself in an open letter, saying: 'I wish to explain to the readers of *Revolución* that I am ill, that I did not catch my illness in gambling dens or spending nights in cabarets, but by working more than my system could endure, for the Revolution. The doctors recommended a house in a place removed from my daily business... I was forced to live in a house that belonged to representatives of the old regime because my salary of $125.00 as an officer of the Rebel Army does not permit me to rent one sufficiently large to house the people who accompany me.'

Che was far from idle at Tarará. He began writing the official history of the war, which naturally stressed the importance of the fighting in the Sierra over the struggle in the cities. This became his handbook *Guerrilla Warfare*. Among other things this told the young revolutionary of the importance of proper footware and the usefulness of carrying a pipe 'as it allows one to make full use of tobacco from cigarettes, at times of scarcity, or whatever is left of cigar stubs.' There were, of course, more profound lessons to be learnt:

We consider that the Cuban Revolution contributed three fundamental things to the conduct of revolutionary movements in America. They are:

1.Popular forces can win a war against the army.

2.It is not necessary to wait for all the conditions for making a revolution to exist; the insurrectional *foco* [guerrilla group] with create them.

3.In the underdeveloped Americas the struggle should take place in the countryside (rather than in the cities as old-fashioned Marxist-Leninists maintained).

At Tarará, there were also meetings of a shadow government, including members of the PSP, which began developing alternative policies to the pro-American showpiece in Havana. Che was in charge of land reforms and planned the revolutionary agency which would implement the policy. It would be called the Instituto Nacional de Reforma Agraria, or INRA.

Together with Raúl he set up a state security apparatus called the *Seguridad del Estado*, or G-2. And he met other Latin Americans and organized attempts to export revolution to Nicaragua, Panama, Haiti, and the Dominican Republic. These small *Granma*-style invasions were fiascos and only served to embarrass Castro when he visited the US in April—a visit Che had opposed.

Indeed President Eisenhower contrived to be out of town playing golf in Georgia during Fidel's visit to Washington. And though he was popular with the press and the people he met on his spontaneous walkabouts—his beard and fatigues adding considerably to his charisma—his meeting with Vice-President Richard Nixon did not go well. The administration considered him either a Communist or incredibly naïve about the Communist influence in his cabinet. Moscow had come to the same view and they thought the way to Fidel was through Che. Likewise, Washington considered Guevara their number-one opponent in Havana. Indeed, Che was against the selling of Coca-Cola, sneakers and American cigarettes in Cuba—even those brands that were made there. Che was even angry when a KGB man gave him a pack of *Tejas*—'Texas'—cigarettes from Argentina.

'*Tejas*, you know what that is?' he said. 'It's the half of Mexico the Yankee bandits stole.'

As always, Che was loyal to the old Spanish empire and resented the dominance of the Anglo-Americans.

Castro had taken his own seaside villa, six miles away at Cojímar where, with Che and Raúl, he planned to unite the 26th of July movement and the PSP into a single revolutionary party. But while the others kept quite about their revolutionary goals, Guevara spoke out publicly on his radical ideas for land reforms, the nationalization of US assets, and the export of revolution to the rest of the Americas.

'The entire Cuban nation should become a guerrilla army,' he said.

In his eyes, the Cuban Revolution had showed that a small body of men, who were supported by the people and who were not afraid of dying, could overcome a disciplined regular army. He called on the other peoples of Latin America to stand up and fight to overthrow their dictators and the monopolistic foreign companies that supported them. This was little short of declaring war on the interests of the United States.

Meanwhile Castro was staging a new revolution of his own, forcing a cabinet split which caused Cardona to resigned. Castro replaced him as prime minister, but only after the law was changed taking the age limit for holding ministerial office down from thirty-five to thirty—Castro was still only thirty-two, while Che was thirty.

A radical land-reform bill was passed in May 1959, causing the share prices of United Fruit and other US companies holding land on Cuba to plummet on Wall Street. In the resulting protests, Urrutia resigned on July 26 to be replaced by Osvaldo Dorticós, a docile *fidelísta*. Castro now took a firmer hand. He cracked down on press freedom after the humorous paper *Zig Zag* satirized him. Students at Havana University were urged to purge 'corrupting influences.' He denounced calls for Cuba to support the US in the Cold War as 'imperialist.' And, with the economic reforms he was proposing, Castro was soon boasting that the standard of living in Cuba would outstrip that of the US in a couple of years. In fact, as Batista had fled with most of Cuba's foreign reserves, the economy was practically a basket case and the middle-classes were heading for Miami.

On May 22, 1959, Che had been granted a divorce from Hilda and on June 2 he married Aleida, who proceeded to give him four children—two girls, two boys. Although she was probably pregnant at the time of her wedding, Aleida wore white. Conscious of his image, Che wore combat green with his trademark a black beret. Their witness was Raúl. There was a party at La Cabaña and it was enlivened by Camilo who brought a couple of bottles of rum.

Concerned to prevent a confrontation with the US before he was ready, Castro had long dreamt of ridding himself of Che, who he had once dismissed as a 'foreign mercenary.' The excuse was an invitation from President Gamal Abdel Nasser of Egypt, who was hosting a celebration on the third anniversary of the nationalization of the Suez Canal. Che was sent as Cuba's representative. Castro even predicted that on his trip to the Middle East, Guevara would suffer a bad attack of asthma.

To prolong his pain, on June 5, Castro told Che that he was sending him on a prolonged foreign trip to the Middle East, Japan, Indonesia, Pakistan, Ceylon (Sri Lanka), and Yugoslavia. He would be away and out of Castro's hair for three months. Castro told him to take Aleida with him, so they could have some sort of honeymoon. Che declined, believing that revolutionary leaders needed to practice austerity in their personal lives.

He spent two weeks in Egypt, seeing the sights and forging a close bond with Nasser, who himself hadturned to the Soviet Union for support. The US government thought that the trip had gone well, but Che managed to offend Nasser when he asked how many Egyptians had fled the country since he took over. Nasser replied not many, and most them had been naturalized Egyptians of foreign origins.

'That means your revolution had not accomplished much,' said Che. 'I measure the depth of change by the number of people it affects, who feel that there is no place for them in the new society.'

In India, he spent twelve days, seeing the sights of the Taj Mahal and Agra, visiting research centers and airplane factories, and witnessing the squalor and poverty of Calcutta. Castro was almost right, but it was the stifling heat of India that brought on an asthma attack. Nevertheless in the Chilean ambassador's house in Delhi, Che stood on his head to demonstrate his knowledge of yoga.

He had dinner with the Indian prime minister Pandit Nehru and his daughter, future prime minister Indira, in the viceroy's palace, but the wily Nehru would not be drawn into any political discussion.

'Mr Prime Minister, what is your opinion of Communist China?' asked Che.

Without a flicker, Nehru replied: 'Mr *Comandante*, have you tasted one of these delicious apples?'

Che tried again.

'Mr Prime Minister, have you read any Mao Tse-tung?'

'Mr *Comandante*,' Nehru replied, 'how pleased I am that you have liked the apples.'

The evening was not a success.

He made a better impression in Japan, though the visit was nearly a disaster. The Cuban ambassador had arranged for Che to lay a wreath on Japan's Tomb of the Unknown soldier, commemorating the men lost in World War II. Che refused saying 'that was an imperialist army that killed millions of Asians.' However, he did agree to go to Hiroshima, 'where the Americans killed 100,000 Japanese.'

His twelve-day trip took him to factories and ports. The secret of Japan's success, he concluded, was willpower and he saw no reason why Cuba could not develop an iron and steel industry. He also went up Mount Fuji and to see sumo wrestling. But he refused to visit a famous cabaret in Osaka, which boasted six hundred women performers and was said to the be largest in the world, ordering the uniformed men in his entourage to stay away too. The civilians could go if they did not mind 'having a *Time* photographer take their picture and create a scandal, showing how the members of the Cuban delegation spend the people's money partying and getting drunk with whores.'

But he was not so strict. When a couple of his men slipped out to visit prostitutes, he admitted that he had 'whored around in my youth.' He also admitted that, when he had been at sea, he had kept a whore in his cabin until he grew tired of her. In a geisha house, he got drunk on sake and tried to ape the geisha girls' dance.

When he ran low on cigars, he confiscated the rest of the delegation's supply, though he shared them with one of his elderly companions. And on evenings in, he made big plans for the future.

'There's a high plain in South America,' he said, 'there in Bolivia and Paraguay, bordering Brazil, Uruguay, Peru and Argentina—if we inserted a guerrilla force there, we could spread the revolution all over South America.'

In Indonesia, President Sukarno regaled him with tales of his sybaritic lifestyle. He had a considerable harem, but his current favorite was a Russian—a 'gift' from the Soviet premier Nikita Krushchev, he said. The following day, after Sukarno had shown him around his huge art collection, Guevara asked why they had not seen 'the little Russian girl, who they say is the best thing in your collection.' The Argentine ambassador, who was acting as translator, almost passed out, but quickly fabricated a question about the Indonesian economy. They had a good laugh about it afterwards.

Despite Sukarno's far from revolutionary lifestyle, Guevara praised him as a 'genuine national hero, who interpreted the popular will and the true needs of the people and denied the counter-revolutionaries the right to sow discord and attack the regime which is the expression of the people's armed struggle.' According to Che, Sukarno was right up there with Nehru, Nasser, and Castro. In fact, the corrupt regime of Sukarno was more like Batista's than Castro's new regime in Cuba.

*

Sukarno was born on June 6, 1901 in Surabaja, Java, when Indonesia was still a Dutch colony. During the 1920s and 1930s, he came to prominence as a nationalist politician seeking independence, founding the Indonesian Nationalist Party in 1928. As a result, he spent two years in a Dutch jail and eight in exile. When the Japanese invaded in 1942, Sukarno welcomed them as liberators, acting as their chief adviser and recruiting labor, soldiers, and 'comfort women' for them.

When the Japanese left at the end of World War II, Sukarno was persuaded to declare Indonesia's independence. The Dutch were finally forced to concede sovereignty in 1949 and Sukarno quickly established himself in the governor-general's lavish palace. He easily won the first presidential election, but his government became notoriously corrupt.

After extracting a billion dollars worth of aid from the US, he switched sides in the Cold War and took a billion dollars more from the Soviet Union. Meanwhile, inflation soared. In 1959 he dissolved parliament and in 1963 declared himself president for life. He became increasingly fearful of a military coup and in 1965 he approved a Communist-backed plot to kidnap six top army generals who were then tortured, mutilated and murdered. General Suharto, commander of the Jakarta garrison, reacted by slaughtering more than 300,000 Communist suspects. He gradually took over power, forcing Sukarno to retire in 1968. On June 21, 1970, he died of kidney failure in Jakarta.

*

Che's visits to Pakistan and Ceylon were uneventful and largely devoted to sightseeing. Yugoslavia was the only Socialist country he visited, though its leader Josip Tito had split with Stalin in 1948 and tried to remain neutral during the Cold War. Che was critical of the 'wide margin of freedom' and 'very great freedom of criticism' allowed in 'an avowedly Communist country' and was appalled that only fifteen per cent of land had been collectivized. After a long lunch at the Brioni National Park in Croatia, he asked Tito for arms. Tito refused, saying that they did not have enough themselves. Two days later Che discovered that Tito had sold arms to an Arab nation. 'Great neutrality,' he exclaimed.

While Che was away Castro summoned Aleida to his office several times to make a long distance call to her husband. Again he offered to send her to him, but he was adamant.

Although Guevara had indulged his desire to travel and enjoyed, once again, being away from his wife and any domestic obligations—he even started writing to his mother again—his trip accomplished nothing—no treaties, trade agreements or arms deals. On September 10, 1959, he returned to his office at the INRA overlooking the Plaza de la Revolución. His one problem was that both Hilda and Aleida worked in the building. There were frequent rows.

While Che had been away, Castro had asked the US to up its Cuban sugar import quota, effectively taking Cuba's entire output. When this was turned down, Castro argued that he was now essentially free to sell his sugar wherever he liked—including to the Soviet Union. This prompted a CIA-backed bombing raid on a sugar refinery. Nevertheless, Castro was still trying to maintain cordial relations with the US. He was preparing to address a convention of two thousand American travel agents with the aim of encouraging tourism when a plane appeared overhead dropping leaflets urging him to purge the Communists from his government. The army opened fire. Che's guard wanted to race up to the roof and open fire, but Che would not give his permission, though he admitted that the leaflets would do more damage than any bomber. A plump secretary took cover under her desk and it took an age to prize her free. The travel agents left town without the benefit of Castro's oratory. The convention was a public relations fiasco and there was a demonstration outside the American embassy, accusing the US of staging a bombing raid— though any casualties there had been were probably caused by indiscriminate anti-aircraft fire.

The US government were not pleased to hear of Che's return. They were even less happy when he took over as director of the National Bank. According to Che, this had happened by accident. Castro had asked whether anyone present was a good '*economista*.' Che said he thought Castro had asked if anyone was a good 'Communista'. In fact, Castro had little other choice. Camilo Cienfuegos had disappeared when his plane went missing over the sea. There were theories that Castro had done away with him because he was too popular, which Che plainly discounted. But Raúl took over as defense minister and Che was the only other person Fidel could trust to run the economy.

Although he knew little of economics outside his reading of Marx, Guevara was organized and disciplined. He took courses in mathematics, economics and, later, Russian. Arriving at his desk mid-morning in his green fatigues, he worked until two or three the following morning in the bank's business. Left wing sympathizers from America and Europe, including Jean-Paul Sartre and Simone de Beauvoir, would be invited to his office at midnight to share cigars and maté with him. He would sit with his feet on the desk, or lie on the floor where it was cooler. Cuban bank notes were signed informally 'Che.'

Around that time the true nature of the regime revealed itself. Huber Matos, leader of the anti-Communist wing of the 26th of July movement, joined the wealthy cattlemen of Camagüey and publicly denounced the growing influence of the PSP in the INRA and the army. In November 1959, he was discharged from the military and charged with treason. The evidence against—gossip, intercepted letters, wiretaps and anonymous accusations—had been gathered by G-2. Found guilty of conspiring against the Revolution, he was sentenced to thirty years. Raúl and Che had demanded the death penalty but, after talking to Matos' relatives, Che changed his mind, even suggesting that Matos lodge an appeal. But anyone else siding with Matos was summarily fired, while a number of 'counter-revolutionaries' were executed. The firing squads had begun again.

Although Che was also involved in diplomacy and the expansion of the Cuban army at the same time, in the fourteen months he ran the National Bank he made a good fist of it by all accounts. However, he did make some serious mistakes. He wanted to pull out of the International Monetary Fund, when paying back their IMF loan would have almost wiped out their reserves of foreign currency and he cut the salaries of the Bank's employees. When told they would leave, he said: 'I don't care, let them leave. We will bring in longshoremen or cane cutters.'

Unfortunately, these manual laborers turned out not to have the skills required and Guevara was forced to change his mind. He also 'intervened' in, then expropriated, factories, putting teenage guerrillas in to run them. This was part of his plan to create a 'guerrilla society.' The problem was eighty per cent of his troops were illiterate.

Che was not above a little uninformed meddling himself. He summoned the architect of the new thirty-two-storey National Bank building on Havana's seafront, the Malecón, and accused him of being 'petit bourgeois,' to which the architect replied no, he was a *gran* bourgeois, his shopkeeper was petit bourgeois.

'You are the only honest person of your class I have met since I got here,' said Che.

'The problem is you don't give them a chance to speak,' the architect replied. This wiped the smile from Guevara's face and he reminded the architect to remember he was speaking to *Comandante* Guevara.

Reviewing the plans of the bank, Che decided that there should be no elevators as they would have to be provided by the US company Otis. If he could climb thirty-two floors with his asthma, he argued, anyone could. Next he cut the number of lavatories by half. When the architect pointed out that even in revolutions people go to the toilet just as much as they did before, Che said: 'Not the new man, he can sacrifice.'

The bank was never built and the site was eventually used for a hospital.

Later the architect, who had supplied maps to the guerrillas when they were in Escambray, went to complain to Che when a friend from the *Juventud Católica* had been put in front of a firing squad for distributing anti-Communist leaflets. Che told him that this may have been unjust but it was 'sanitary' and the architect was warned to leave the island or face a firing squad too. He fled. Another INRA employee fled after being accused of being a counter-revolutionary for 'speaking ill' of Che's wife.

In Guevara's eyes moderates were the real enemy.

'"Moderation" is another one of those words colonial agents like to use,' he said. 'All those who are afraid or who are considering some form of treason are moderates.'

Although he was a Communist, Che was not overly ideological when it came to Marxist economics. He was more interested in politics and he took a hard line, which took the regime further to the left and forced a gradual break with America.

While Che courted the Soviet Union, all US farms were seized, without compensation, and turned into collectives. When Washington's complaints of other nonpayment and illegal seizures were ignored, the US cancelled its order for Cuban sugar, so a buyer was sought elsewhere. And on February 3, 1960, Soviet Deputy Prime Minister Anastas Mikoyan paid a visit. He was accompanied by Che's old friend from Mexico City, KGB man Nikolai Leonov. He brought a chess set for Raúl and 'for Che, who likes arms, we brought two weapons: a very fine pistol and another high-precision sports model, along with ammunition.'

Mikoyan met Castro at Fidel's fishing cottage. But according to another KGB man present at the meeting 'Che was the principal architect of Soviet-Cuban economic co-operation.'

Leonov said that he was present at the key conversations between Mikoyan and Castro. Mikoyan had authority to offer the Cubans a loan of $100 million. Castro said that was not enough to restructure the economy.

Mikoyan said: 'Well, let's use the $100 million and then we'll go on talking and get more.'

'When taking a historic step it is better to have a far deeper commitment,' said Che. 'It is no joke reorienting a country from one side to the other. If you drop us halfway with $100 or $200 million, we won't solve anything.'

An ambassador to Moscow was appointed and an oil-for-sugar deal concluded. At the time, the Cubans did not ask for arms. But they did the following month, after the French ship *La Coubre* carrying a shipment of Belgian rifles and ammunition blew up in Havana harbor, killing over 100 Cubans. Che boarded the burning ship to help rescue the injured. The following day he and Castro led the funeral cortege along the Malecón. And when Castro made a two-hour speech from a balcony, a young photographer named Alberto Korda snapped Che standing beside him. This was to be the famous image of Che that is seen worldwide to this day, though it was not published at the time.

'I was slightly below the level of the dais with a 9mm Leica camera,' said Korda. 'I used my small telephoto lens and took all the people in the first row: Fidel, Jean-Paul Sartre, and Simone de Beauvoir. Che was not visible. He was standing behind the rostrum. But for a moment there was an empty space in the front row, and in the background the figure of Che appeared. He unexpectedly entered my viewfinder and I shot the photo horizontally. I immediately realized that the image of him was almost a portrait, with the clear sky behind him… It all happened in less than ten or fifteen seconds. Che left and didn't appear again. It was a coincidence.'

Later Castro cabled Krushchev asking him to send arms secretly. But Krushchev was not afraid of ruffling the feathers of the US and replied that he would send arms openly.

US-owned oil refineries refused to refine Soviet oil, so Che refused to pay them monies that were owed. When the oil companies still refused to back down they were expropriated. Che drew up the nationalization decree. He considered this his first victory over the US, and he had done it with Soviet help.

When Washington finally announced that it would buy no more sugar from Cuba, Khrushchev said that the Soviet Union would take the US quota. But this quota, Che had always argued, meant 'economic slavery' for the Cuban people. By paying above market prices for sugar, the US made Cuba maintain a single-crop economy, stopping it diversifying and keeping the country dependent on US imports. But Cuba was now a pawn in a much bigger game of diplomacy. Two weeks earlier, the Soviets had fallen out with Communist China. Coming to the aid of Cuba was the perfect way for the Soviet Union to show that it still supported the international struggle, while withdrawing its support from China.

At the height of the conflict with the US, Krushchev announced that he would defend Cuba with missiles if necessary. Che was over the moon.

'Cuba is now... a glorious island in the centre of the Caribbean, defended by the missiles of the greatest military power in history,' he wrote.

But the Cubans soon backed down. Castro announced that Cuban independence rested on the justice of its cause, not Soviet weapons and Che concurred that they would fight to the last man to stop Cuba becoming a Soviet satellite. Nevertheless, Che was named head of the regime's first delegation to the Soviet Union in October 1960. In the meantime, he instigated a Soviet-style measure in Cuba, setting up the first labor camp on the remote Guanahacabibes Peninsula at the western tip of the island. It would house political dissidents and, later, homosexuals and AIDS victims.

'We only send to Guanahacabibes those doubtful cases where we are not sure people should go to jail,' said Guevara. 'I believe that people who should go to jail should go to jail anyway. Whether long-standing militants or whatever, they should go to jail. We send to Guanahacabibes those people who should not go to jail, people who have committed crimes against revolutionary morals, to a greater or lesser degree, along with simultaneous sanctions like being deprived of their posts, and in other cases not those sanctions, but rather be reeducated through labor. It is hard labor, not brute labor, rather the working conditions are hard but not brutal.'

All opposition newspapers were closed down or taken over. The editor of *Bohemia* Miguel Ángel Quevedo, who had once compared Castro to Christ, shut down his magazine and fled the country after complaining that he had reduced Cuba to a state of 'Russian vassalage.' Unions were purged and Che told the universities that the state was going to design a new curriculum to help the country industrialize.

'Who has the right to say that only ten lawyers should graduate a year and that a hundred industrial chemists should graduate a year?' he asked. 'That is dictatorship, and all right, it is dictatorship.'

Cuba needed 'a great army of those who do, leaving by the wayside that small patrol of those who talk.' They should follow his example and give up their individual vocations for the sake of the Revolution. He also told the universities that they 'must paint themselves black, mulatto, worker, and peasant.' If not, the people would break down the doors and 'paint the university the colors they liked.'

Independently minded professors left the country, followed by liberals and anti-Communists from the 26th of July movement. Some dissidents returned to the Escambray, burning sugar crops and murdering literacy workers. Meanwhile the US armed the exiles who had washed up in Miami and began to plan the Bay of Pigs.

A rumor circulated that Fidel was seriously ill and that Che had taken over in a palace coup. Soon after, *Time* magazine put Guevara on its cover, claiming that Che was the brains of the Revolution, while Fidel was his heart and Raúl its fist.

'Wearing a smile of melancholy sweetness that many women find devastating, Che guides Cuba with an icy calculation, vast competence, high intelligence and a perceptive sense of humor,' said *Time*.

By this time, though, the world's favorite revolutionary had moved into a pretty two-story house in a middle-class suburb and Aleida was expecting their first child. His salary was $1,000 a month, through he took only $250 as the salary of a *comandante*. This meant that those under him had to take a voluntary pay cut too. However, Che enjoyed other perks. In the bank he had a private dining room—which he himself dismissed as *bourgeois*—where he entertained old friends such as Alberto Granado, who had come from Venezuela with his family for a visit and decided to stay. Granado, and others, noticed that Che was putting on weight, especially on his face. Che denied this was because of the comfortable lifestyle he was leading and blamed it on the cortisone he was then taking for his asthma.

By that time, Soviet arms and military advisers were arriving in Cuba. They even sent tanks. Castro warned of the threat of imminent invasion and introduced the slogan '*Cuba Sí, Yanqui No!*' He also discounted the prospect of elections, since the people already ruled Cuba and he soon had the crowds yelling '*Revolución Sí, Elecciones No!*'

Che was also contemptuous of elections. Western Communist parties' policy of a peaceful parliamentary strategy to gain power 'would deliver the working class bound hand and foot over to the ruling class,' he said.

The Cuban army had already doubled in number to 50,000 since the Revolution. Another 50,000 had joined the people's militia and former Batista army officers were warning the US Senate that the Soviets were building missile sites on the island. Che had already embraced the idea of atomic war. Speaking for the Cuban people, he told the First Latin American Youth Congress: 'This people you see today tell you that even if they should disappear from the face of the earth because an atomic war is unleashed in their name… they would feel completely happy and fulfilled if each one of you, upon reaching your lands, can say: "Here we are. Our words come moist from the Cuban jungles. We have climbed the Sierra Maestra and we have known the dawn, and our minds and our hands are full with the seed of the dawn, and we are prepared to sow it in this land and to defend it so that it flourishes."'

Castro had also taken up Che's theme of continent-wide revolution, warning that 'Cuba's example would convert the Andean cordillera into the hemisphere's Sierra Maestra.' The first country on Che's list was Venezuela, then being run by the Socialist Rómulo Betancourt who he had fallen out with in Costa Rica in 1953.

But Guevara had even more radical ideas. He believed that the 'individual... must disappear,' that 'the proper utilization of the whole individual [was for] the absolute benefit of the community,' and that 'a new type of human being should be created.' He would not be gainsaid on his idea of the 'new man.'

When the French Marxist economist René Dumont, who had been brought in to convert the economy from capitalism to socialism, pointed out that workers on the collectives should be paid, so that they had more of a sense of ownership, Che 'reacted violently.' Dumont said that Che had an 'ideal vision of a Socialist Man, who would become a stranger to the mercantile side of things, working for society and not for profit. He was very critical of the industrial success of the Soviet Union, where, he said, everybody works and strives and tries to go beyond his quota, but only to earn more money. He did not think that the Soviet Man was really a new sort of man, for he did not find him any different, really, than a Yankee. He refused to consciously participate in the creation in Cuba "of a second American society."'

Che wanted to skip stages in the evolution of socialism, as Mao had attempted in his Great Leap Forward in China, 1958-1960, where he had attempted to industrialize the country overnight with the massive production of steel.

There was a presidential election in the US in 1960 and Cuba became a hot issue. John F. Kennedy, who had frequently holidayed in Cuba before the Revolution, promised to get tough. Once in the White House he inherited the CIA's plan to invade from the Eisenhower administration and gave it the go-ahead. Meanwhile, Castro annoyed the Americans as much as he could, bear hugging Krushchev and, when visiting the UN, staying at a hotel in Harlem to show solidarity with the oppressed black people of the United States. He then delivered a three-hour speech, the longest every recorded in the General Assembly.

Back in Cuba, Guevara called the island's richest man Julio Lobo in to see him and told him that he must either join the Revolution or leave.

'We are Communists and we cannot allow you to go on as you are, representing the very essence of capitalism,' he said.

If he stayed Che would appoint him administrator of the sugar industry. He would lose his plantations, but he would receive a handsome salary and be allowed to keep one of his houses and the profits from one of his mills. Lobo said he would think it over. Two days later he went into exile in Spain.

It became illegal to own more than one home and all rented property was taken over by the state. The US reacted with a trade embargo on everything except medicine and food. Castro then nationalized all the remaining US companies in Cuba. The cars that those fleeing the country left behind were also nationalized. Che's assistant Orlando Borrego managed to get his hands on a brand-new E-type Jaguar, taken from a cigarette factory he had nationalized. Che did not approve, accusing him of being a pimp. Such an ostentatious car was not suitable for a representative of the people, he said, and Borrego was forced to drive a battered Chevy Impala like his boss.

'Che was super-strict,' said Borrego, 'like Jesus Christ.'

In October 1960, Che went to Prague and then to Moscow, again without Aleida who was eight-months pregnant. His mission was to conclude the sugar deal, but he also wanted to apply to join the Soviet bloc. Another thing on the agenda was the election of John F. Kennedy, who won the presidential race when he was there.

An honored guest, Che stood next to Krushchev in Red Square to review the annual military parade commemorating the October Revolution. He went to the Bolshoi Ballet and traveled to Leningrad (which is now, once again, called St Petersburg) to see the Smolny Institute when Lenin had launched the Bolshevik Revolution, the Hermitage, and the Winter Palace. During his stay, he was not allowed to give his hosts the slip and see how ordinary Russians lived. However, he was a little disconcerted that his hosts ate off the finest china.

'So the proletariat here eats off French porcelain, eh?' he said.

Secretly he was shocked by the luxurious lifestyles of the top Communist officials. It seems that he also noticed how in Prague and Moscow, young women were employed in the hotels to sexually entrap foreign visitors, but he did not seem to object. On the other hand, his hosts were very impressed with his punctuality—'he hardly seemed Latin American at all,' said one. However it was always difficult to entertain him, because of his food allergies.

His hosts were also rather puzzled by his approach to economics. He wanted to industrialize overnight, with a steel plant pumping out a million tons of steel a year. The catastrophic failure of China's Great Leap Forward had done nothing to dampen his ardor. Asked where he was going to keep all that steel, Guevara said that they would build a car plant. But the Soviets pointed out that Cuba was not big enough to support an industrial economy. Besides it had no iron ore to make steel, nor any coal to smelt it. If Cuba needed hard currency, the Soviets told him, like the Americans before them, it should grow sugar. But it was not hard currency that Che was after. He wanted to build an industrial working class, so that a Communist state could flourish along the lines Marx predicted.

Che also did not seem to notice the growing tension between the Soviet Union and China. He traveled on to Beijing, where he met Mao Tse-tung and discussed China's support of Patrice Lumumba's struggle to rid the Congo of its colonial power, Belgium. Che was an instant fan of China, despite its economic difficulties.

'Naturally one cannot pretend that the standard of living in China is like that of developed countries in the capitalist world,' he told a television audience when he got back, 'but there are absolutely none of the symptoms of misery that one sees in other Asian countries which we have had the chance to visit, even far more developed ones like Japan. And one sees that everyone eats, everyone is dressed—dressed uniformly, it's true, but everyone is decently dressed—everybody has work and an extraordinary spirit.'

After two weeks in China, he flew on to North Korea, which he liked even better, saying: 'Of all the Socialist countries we visited in person, Korea is one of the most extraordinary. It is perhaps the one that impressed us most of all.'

The Americans thought that Che had done rather well signing a sugar deal on the trip; but the British thought he had done badly. On his way home he stopped off in Budapest where he made contact with his old friend Fernando Barral, who joined Che in Cuba the following year. Then he went on to East Berlin to do another sugar deal. There he met Argentine-born Tamara 'Tania' Bunka, who was his translator. Later she was invited to Havana 'to keep Che happy' and was killed fighting alongside him in Bolivia. While he was away, Aleida gave birth to a daughter, who was also named Aleida.

Back in Cuba, he threw himself into voluntary work, unloading Soviet ships and cutting sugar cane—though the dust triggered asthma attacks. Even so he considered manual labor a pleasure 'done with joy, to the rhythm of revolutionary songs, amid the fraternal camaraderie and human contacts which invigorate and dignify all involved.' This was an idea he had got from China.

Working without remuneration solely for the good of society helped develop Communist consciousness and the image of Che Guevara cutting cane, carrying sacks of rice and digging ditches became part of the iconography of the Revolution. Soon everyone in Cuba was obliged to do 'voluntary' work at weekends. Some enjoyed it; others hated it. And it soon became a way to exploit the workers, upping sugar production while depressing wages.

When Kennedy came into office, he sought to isolate Cuba by giving more aid to Latin America, provided they did not trade with new regime. But Che was not downhearted. He told the Soviet ambassador that 'Latin America is at boiling point and next year we can expect revolutionary explosions in several countries, starting with Peru and Paraguay.' History has shown that this was wishful thinking.

Guevara also believed that the conditions for revolution in other Latin American countries were far better than they had been in Cuba. What they needed were 'truly revolutionary leaders capable of leading the people against their current corrupt and reactionary governments and achieving victory… We must overcome the fatalism that is so widespread among the peoples of Latin American countries, in the sense that it is impossible to fight against American imperialism.'

Cuba's growing links with the Soviet bloc were far from popular in Cuba. While the Americans had brought money, the Soviets had brought their own sandwiches. Seeing the cars, swimming pools and other facilities that the Americans had left behind, trade delegates from Eastern bloc thought that they had arrived in heaven, while Cuban youths sent to study in 'agrarian collectives' in the USSR got the opposite impression. Although American tourists were loud and spoke Spanish badly, the new visitors spoke no Spanish, dressed badly, had little money to spend and smelt bad. They had no deodorants and Cubans were particular about these things. Che had to go on television to apologize for this. He said that he had brought up the question of deodorant production during his Moscow visit, but 'they cannot be bothered with such things. We too now have to occupy ourselves with more important things.'

The learning of English was discouraged. Instead Cuba's second language was to be Russian, though there were no Russian-Spanish text books available. After the Revolution Fidel and Ernesto had been popular names for children, now they were Alexei and Natasha. Public buildings were rechristened with the names of revolutionary heroes—Rosa Luxemburg, Patrice Lumumba and *Los Héroes de Vietnam*. The old Chaplin Cinema on First Avenue became the Carlos Marx. Santa Claus—an American invention—was banned and, eventually, even Christmas was outlawed.

Che was personally blamed for Cuba's 'submission' to the Soviet Union and, around this time, several attempts were made on his life. In one, his house in Miramar was shot up, terrifying Aleida, little Aleida—now known affectionately as Aliusha—and their twenty-five-year-old nanny. Che could hardly be expected to go without domestic servants. As a precaution, he took to carrying a cigar box full of grenades around with him.

Preparations for war were now in full swing. The streets were full of uniformed men and women carrying weapons, and militiamen used pneumatic drills to lay explosives. Che welcomed the coming conflict. Cuba, he believed, was in the vanguard of the anti-colonialist struggle. If it could break free from the imperialist system, others would follow. However, he believed that the US would be too afraid to invade them.

'They know they cannot attack us directly,' he told his staff. 'There are rockets with atomic warheads that can be deployed anywhere.'

According to Guevara, the Americans were 'the new Nazis of the world, [but] they don't even have the tragic greatness of those German generals who thrust all of Europe into the worst holocaust the world has ever known, and destroyed themselves in an apocalyptic ending. These new Nazis, cowardly felons and liars [will be] vanquished by history.'

The US believed that the Soviets were ahead in the arms race and the 'missile gap' featured in the 1960 election. By the end of 1961, US intelligence would determine that America was far ahead of the Soviet Union in nuclear strike capability. But it did not look that way in the spring when, on April 12, Yuri Gagarin became the first man into space. Che was convinced that the future belonged to Communism. Later that year Gagarin came to Cuba to celebrate the 26 July raid.

On April 14, 1961, Havana's largest department store was burnt to the ground by CIA-backed guerrillas. The following morning an air raid destroyed most of the Cuba air force on the ground. Che was awoken by the nanny. He headed for Pinar del Río, where he took command of the Western Army. Just after midnight on April 17, 1,500 Cuban exiles arrived off the south side of the island on a ship lent to them by the United Fruit Company with a US Navy escort. They came ashore at Playa Girón in the Bay of Pigs.

The landings had initially been planned for a beach near the city of Trinidad, but Kennedy suggested they land somewhere more discrete. But the Bay of Pigs was a ludicrous landing site as inland lay the huge Zapata swamp. Castro knew the place well. He liked to go fishing there. Unable to move inland, they dug in on the beaches and waited for support from the guerrillas who had returned to the Escambray mountains. None came. The CIA had not informed the Cuban resistance in case of a leak. As it was, Castro rounded up the dissidents, then rode into battle on a Soviet tank. Kennedy was informed that, unless the US intervened, the invading army of exiles would be wiped out. He refused, authorizing only minimal air support.

Although Che took no part in the action, he was wounded when his pistol fell out of his holster and went off. The bullet grazed his cheek. He was then given an antitetanus injection that brought on anaphylactic shock.

'My friends almost managed to do what my enemies couldn't,' said Che. 'I almost died.'

And he wore his wound with pride.

On April 19, the invaders' last position was taken, 114 of them were dead and over 1,100 taken prisoner. Returning from hospital in Havana, Che drove to the Bay of Pigs, where he interrogated the prisoners. One

Che Guevara: The Last Conquistador

of them was so frightened at the sight of Che he pissed and shat in his pants. The man was too frightened to speak and Che ordered his bodyguard to get him a bucket of water. The prisoners were eventually sold back to Kennedy for $53 million in food and medicine.

Four months later in Uruguay, Che met twenty-nine-year-old White House aide Richard Goodwin and said: 'Thank you for the Playa Girón. Before the invasion the Revolution was shaky. Now, it is stronger than ever.'

This consolidation was done by the most brutal means. During the invasion, 100,000 anti-Castro 'conspirators' were rounded up and held in the La Cabaña fortress, Príncipe Castle, the Blanquita Theatre, and Matanzas baseball stadium. Their leaders were shot. Che was delighted. He told the Soviet ambassador: 'Cuba's counterespionage agencies are going to repress the counterrevolutionaries in a decisive way, not allowing them to raise their head again as before the attack.'

As a result the PSP, the Revolutionary Student Organization and the 26th of July movement were fused together to form the United Party of the Socialist Revolution. But Che was soon critical of some of the new party's leaders who 'enjoyed various privileges—beautiful secretaries, Cadillac cars, and air-conditioning keeping the warm Cuban atmosphere outside.'

By this time, Che was minister of industries and responsible for the whole of the Cuban economy. When he moved into the ministry, he told his secretary: 'We are going to spend five years here and then we will go. When we are five years older, we will still be able to do guerrilla warfare.'

163

With the Revolution now secure, Guevara was in a position to undertake some radical social engineering. Key to this was the economy. As Krushchev had decreed a policy of peaceful coexistence with the United States, the two superpowers competed economically with Krushchev threatening to 'bury' America with steel production—then thought to be a key indicator of prosperity.

Having heeded the warning of the Cuban revolution, the Kennedy administration instituted a 'Latin-American Marshall Plan,' giving $20 billion in aid to countries that made the kind of liberal reforms that would quell further guerrilla uprisings. A conference instigating the program was to be held at Punta del Este in Uruguay. Che was going to attend in any attempt to scupper the American plan by flaunting the aid that Cuba was receiving from the Soviet Union.

Punta del Este is a beach resort just across the mouth of the River Plate from Argentina, so Che's mother, aunt, brothers and sisters, and numerous old friends came to visit him. He enquired after people he loved, particularly Chichina and her uncles. But he fell out with his brother Roberto, who had married an Argentinian aristocrat and was a lawyer from the Argentine navy. Che criticized him for 'serving an instrument of oppression' and pointed to his own draft-dodging because he was not willing 'to serve in the armed forces of a corrupt regime that was an ally of American imperialism.' Roberto found his brother humorless, though others remember him joking with them, especially at a large family dinner.

Argentina's new leftwing magazine called itself *Che*, but its editor, Julia Constenla de Giussani, found Guevara in the flesh both arrogant and mean spirited. Otherwise he was hero worshipped. Traveling again without Aleida, women threw themselves at him. Even Julia Constenla de Giussani admitted: 'As a person he had an incalculable enchantment that was completely natural. If he entered a room, everything began to revolve around him… He was blessed with a unique appeal.' And she looked after him one afternoon when his asthma got the better of him.

In the conference hall itself, Che was 'masterful.' He repeatedly reminded the other Latin American delegates that they should thank the Cuban Revolution for any assistance they were receiving from the US— these monies 'bear the name of Cuba whether their beneficiaries like it or not.' But despite Guevara's revolutionary bluster, he was conciliatory towards the US, even agreeing to cooperate with the regional organizations they were setting up. As to exporting revolution, Guevara said: 'We cannot stop exporting an example, as the United States wishes, because an example is something that transcends borders. What we do give is a guarantee that we will not export revolutions, we guarantee that not a single rifle will leave Cuba, that not a single weapon will leave Cuba for battle in any other country of America.'

This was an out-and-out lie and all the more surprising as observers 'had almost expected Guevara to mow down the delegates with his machine gun; they hoped he would call for a continental uprising, and curse the day the United States had been born.'

But Guevara was there to laud the economic success of the Revolution.

'The growth rate cited as a great success for all America is 2.5 per cent,' he said. 'We are speaking of a rate of development [for Cuba] of 10 per cent without the slightest doubt… What are Cuba's plans for 1980? Well, a per capita income of $3,000, more than the United States today… They should leave us alone; let us develop, and in twenty years we'll come here again, and we'll see whether the swan song was revolutionary Cuba's, or their own.'

The message was not universally well received. One heckler shouted '*Asesino*'—'murderer'—at him before being dragged out by security guards, while two others scaled the podium to deliver a barrage of insults. Later a shot was fired when he gave a speech at the University of Montevideo and a professor was killed. A CIA plot to assassinate him was suspected.

Che even sought bilateral talks with the US, beginning the process by delivering two boxes of cigars to Richard Goodwin—one for him and one for President Kennedy. As Cuba intended to vote against the final declaration, protocol ruled out any meeting while the conference was going on. But afterwards Che met Goodwin at a party in the home of a Brazilian diplomat in Montevideo.

'Che was wearing green fatigues and his usual overgrown and scraggly beard,' said Goodwin. 'Behind the beard his features are quite soft, almost feminine, and his manner is intense. He has a good sense of humor, and there was considerable joking back and forth during the meeting. He seemed very ill at ease when we began to talk, but soon became relaxed and spoke freely. Although he left no doubt of his personal and intense devotion to Communism, his conversation was free of propaganda and bombast. He spoke calmly, in a straightforward manner, and with the appearance of detachment and objectivity. He left no doubt, at any time, that he felt completely free to speak for his government and rarely distinguished between his personal observations and the official position of the Cuban government. I had the definite impression that he had thought out his remarks very carefully—they were extremely well organized.'

Again, according to Goodwin, 'all the women at the party swarmed around him,' then 'one of the Brazilians said Che had something important to say.' They spoke for around half-an-hour. Che was frank. The Cuban revolution was socialist in nature and irreversible, he said. However, the trade embargo was causing them financial problems. Cuba sought a rapprochement with the US. In return, they would pay for US assets they had confiscated and promised not to enter into any military or political alliances with the Soviet bloc, nor to attack the US Navy base at Guantánamo, and hold elections once the 'single party' had been institutionalized.

Goodwin wrote a memorandum for Kennedy recommending reconciliation with Cuba. However, at the time Rómulo Betancourt was under pressure from leftwing guerrillas. Any détente with Cuba would look like a victory for Castro and risked a coup in Venezuela. The world was now more divided than ever. Directly after the Punta del Este conference, the Berlin Wall went up.

That summer Kennedy did read Che Guevara's *Guerrilla Warfare* and decided to form a new counterinsurgency force, formally endorsing the Green Berets. This was at the same time as hundreds of Argentinians, Bolivians, Chileans, Colombians, Guatemalans, Nicaraguans, Peruvians, Uruguayans, and Venezuelans flocked to Cuba to be taught the art of guerrilla warfare by Che Guevara.

*

A designated Special Forces unit had been set up at Fort Bragg, North Carolina in 1952 and from 1953 its troops wore their distinctive green berets when they went in to the field, although the US Army refused to authorize its official use. However, when President Kennedy visited Fort Bragg on 12 October 1961, he sent word to the Special Warfare Center commander, Brigadier General William P. Yarborough, that all Special Forces soldiers wear their green berets during his inspection. Afterwards the president told the Pentagon that he considered the green beret to be 'symbolic of one of the highest levels of courage and achievement of the United States military.' Soon, the green beret became synonymous with Special Forces and the two terms became interchangeable.

There were already three Special Forces groups, one based at Bad Tolz in West Germany, one in Fort Bragg, and one in the Far East. A green beret, Captain Harry G. Cramer Jr. of the 14th Special Forces Detachment, had become the first American soldier to die in Vietnam on October 21 1956. Throughout the late 1950s and early 1960s, the number of Special Forces military advisers in Vietnam increased steadily. Their job was to train South Vietnamese soldiers in the art of counterinsurgency and to mould minority tribes into anticommunist forces.

In September 1964, the green berets' 5th Group set up its headquarters in Nha Trang, where it remained until it returned to Fort Bragg in 1971, although some Special Forces teams stayed in Thailand from where they launched secret missions into Vietnam. During the 1960s, other Special Forces training teams were operating in Bolivia, Venezuela, Guatemala, Columbia and the Dominican Republic. Counterinsurgency groups in Latin America carried out some 450 clandestine operations against guerrilla forces between 1965 and 1968. And in 1968, the green berets were involved in tracking down and capturing Che Guevara, in the wilds of south-central Bolivia. By then the green berets had already taken their place in American mythology. In 1966 Barry Sadler's 'The Ballad of the Green Beret' went to number one in the US and in 1968 John Wayne starred in the movie *The Green Berets*. The green berets' A-teams—twelve-man teams comprising two officers, two operations and intelligence sergeants, two weapons sergeants, two communications sergeants, two medics, and two engineers, all trained in unconventional warfare, cross-trained in each others' specialities, and speaking at least one foreign language—were later celebrated in a long-running US TV series.

*

After the conference, Che flew secretly to Buenos Aires where he had a meeting with Argentine President Arturo Frondízi. President Kennedy had asked Frondízi to do this in the mistaken belief that Che, though a Communist, was a friend of the US, while Castro was the Soviet's man. Afterwards he ate a steak with Frondízi's wife and daughter, and went to see his aunt for the last time. When news of the visit leaked, a bomb went off outside the apartment building where his uncle lived. Later a bomb was found outside his mother's house too. Seven months after Che's visit, President Frondízi was ousted in a military coup.

Next Guevara went to Brasilia, where Brazilian President Janio Quadros decorated him with the prestigious Orden Cruzeiro do Sol. Che was extremely uncomfortable with the ceremony and, afterwards, the decoration was taken off and returned. Nevertheless, five days later, Quadros was also ousted in a military coup. Other Latin American countries got the message and began cutting off diplomatic relations with Cuba.

The CIA then began a new $50-million program called Operation Mongoose. Its aim was to destabilize Cuba, where there were already food shortages and rationing of cooking oil and soap. Officially, this was blamed on the US trade embargo. In fact, domestic production was down and people began to blame the restructuring of the economy and the flight of the management class for their plight.

This economic downturn was all the more unfortunate as Che himself had made the state of the economy the yardstick of the success of the Revolution at the Punta del Este conference. At home too, Che set unrealistic economic targets. Castro later commented that Che was always one step ahead of the beat, both on the dance floor and in history.

Despite the economic downturn, nothing was to get in the way of Che's ambitious four-year plan: 'The adoption of a growth rate of 15 per cent to be self-sufficient by 1965 in food and agricultural raw materials... ; to multiply ten-fold production of fruits and other raw materials for the canning industry... ; to build 25,000 rural homes and 25,000 to 30,000 urban homes... ; to reach full employment within the first year of the plan... ; to keep consumer and wholesale prices stable; to attain a harvest of 9.4 million tons of sugar by 1965; to achieve an overall growth of food consumption by 12 per cent annually...'

In other words, Che said he was going to double living standards in just four years. Education and health provisions would be extended to the whole population. Goods formerly imported would be produced domestically and consumption would increase, while sugar production continued to climb.

Che was no economist. Even as a politician he was a dreamer and his unrealistic plan only helped hasten Cuba's economic collapse. There were successes though. Cuba's illiteracy rate was slashed. Hospitals and clinics were built and huge numbers of doctors trained to replace those who had fled to Miami. This was done at the expense of consumer goods and Cuba's foreign currency reserves. The only way Cuba could earn foreign currency was to sell sugar, but the land under cultivation was actually reduced as Che tried to diversify the economy. Besides Cuba had lost its biggest customer who used to pay above market prices—the USA. Meanwhile Che tried building industrial plants, spending money as if the Soviets had extended 'not a $100-million five-year credit but an unlimited account.' Half the fruit and vegetables grown in 1961 and 1962 were left unharvested due to shortages of labor and problems with transport and the canning factories as much of the equipment supplied by the Soviet bloc was substandard, while American machinery rusted in the fields as they could no longer get spare parts. Highly sulphuric Soviet oil corroded the pipes in US-built refineries and the Soviet's metric spanners would not fit US nuts, while Soviet screws could not be used to fix anything because their threads were too uneven.

By March 1962, rationing was extended to milk, eggs, chicken, beef, rice, beans, fish, oil, detergent, and toothpaste. Che had to appear on television and admit that this was his fault as he had devised 'an absurd plan, disconnected from reality, with absurd goals and imaginary resources.'

When in 1962, the Soviets wanted to put forty nuclear missiles on the island of Cuba in retaliation for the deployment of American missiles in Turkey, Che was enthusiastic and went to Krushchev's holiday home on the Black Sea to discuss it with him.

'Anything that can stop the Americans invading is worthwhile,' he said.

And when the Soviets stalled on signing a defense treaty, Che threatened to go public. Krushchev reassured him that if anything went wrong he would send the Baltic Fleet.

Overflights by US spy planes quickly detected the Soviet build-up on the island. Even though the Soviets assured Kennedy that no offensive weapons were being deployed, he called up 150,000 men, giving his own assurances that he did not intend to invade.

Che gave the game away at a reception at the Brazilian embassy. The weapons the Soviets were deploying were not just for the defense of Cuba. They marked a historic shift in the balance of power.

'The United States can do nothing but yield,' he said.

In July 1962, the US learned that missiles were being shipped to Cuba and on August 29 U-2 spy planes spotted the construction of missile sites. The first missile appeared on October 14. President Kennedy weighed the options. He did not know that twenty of the forty-two missiles deployed on Cuba had nuclear warheads—more than enough to obliterate America's eastern seaboard. Nor did he know that the Soviets had also sent 42,000 soldiers and six tactile missile launchers armed with nine missiles with nuclear tips, designed to be used against any invading force. Even so, he ruled out invading the island or bombing the launch sites. Instead, on October 22, he blockaded the island, preventing the delivery of more Soviet missiles.

A shipload were on their way. For six days, the world held its breath, believing that it was on the brink of nuclear war. On October 28, the Soviet ship carrying the missiles turned back. It seemed like a victory for the US. Krushchev agreed to stop construction of the launch sites and withdraw any missiles he had already deployed. However, secretly, Kennedy had promised to withdraw US missiles from Turkey in exchange.

Castro was infuriated. He kicked the wall and called Krushchev a 'sonofabitch, a bastard, an arsehole' who 'had no *cojones*, and the cry went up in Havana: '*Nikita, mariquita, lo que se da no se* quita'— 'Nikita, you poof, what you give, you can't take back'. Castro was eventually placated by an invitation from Krushchev to visit Moscow and renegotiate trade and military deals. The Soviets invited Che to accompany him, but he refused to go.

Che was kept out of the way during the Cuban Missile Crisis. Again he was dispatched to Pinar del Río. But there was no doubt where he stood. In an interview where he alternately puffed on a Cuban cigar and sucked on an asthma inhaler, he told the British Communist Party newspaper the *Daily Worker*—now the *Morning Star*—afterwards: 'If the rockets had remained, we would have used them all and directed them against the very heart of the United States, including New York, in our defense against aggression. But we haven't got them, so we will fight with what we've got.'

When Krushchev backed down, Che was furious. Here was 'the harrowing example of a people ready to sacrifice itself to nuclear arms, that its ashes might serve as a basis for new societies, and when... the atomic missiles are withdrawn, it does not breathe a sigh of relief [in its] determination to struggle, even alone, against all dangers, and even the atomic threat of Yankee imperialism,' he said.

Che told the visiting Soviet Deputy Prime Minister Anastas Mikoyan that the withdrawal of the missiles had undermined those engaged in the struggle and would lead to the 'decline of the revolutionary movement in Latin America.'

Mikoyan replied that they had withdrawn the missiles to prevent Cuba from being destroyed.

'We see your readiness to die beautifully,' he said. 'But we believed that it isn't worth dying beautifully… Socialism must live.'

Things got so tense during this meeting that, when the translator made a slip, Che pulled out his pistol and handed it to him, telling him 'there was only one thing left to do.'

Despite his growing disillusionment with the Soviet Union, Che's revolutionary fervor grew after the Cuban missile crisis and he began to make plans to go and start a revolution in Argentina. It was then that Tamara Burke—Tania—turned up. She was a Stasi informer who was now working for their overseas espionage division. However, a month after she left East Germany, her recruiter defected to the CIA and her cover was blown. The Stasi told her not to go to North or South America. For the time being she stayed on Cuba and trained with Che. The rest of the would-be Argentine revolutionaries had been sent to train in Algeria in case Cuba was invaded.

But the Argentine group began to fall apart and other Communist groups in Latin America wanted nothing to do with the guerrillas Guevara sent them. Mario Monje—head of the Bolivian Communist Party, which had been declared legal after years of repression—told Che: 'You have a machine gun stuck in your brain, and you can't imagine any other way to develop an anti-imperialist struggle.'

Che was itching to take the revolutionary war to the rest of Latin America. But he was now a family man. Aleida had given birth to Camilo in May 1962 and, falling pregnant during the Cuban missile crisis, she had given birth on June 14, 1963—Che's 35th birthday—to a daughter they named Celia, after Che's mother. Meanwhile, Che received news that his mother was in prison in Argentina for her political views—she had become considerably more radical since her Ernestito had become Che.

Although he was the father of four, now on the brink of middle-age, Che still wore the olive-drab fatigues that he had worn in the jungle in a manner so slovenly that any other soldier would have been reprimanded. But he needed to wear his clothing loose in the heat of Cuba due to his asthma. He had, however, shorn his locks and had put on weight. He saw little of his family, preferring to spend his little spare time alone writing in a study that boasted a bust of Lenin and a small statue of Simón Bolívar.

Sometimes on a Sunday afternoon, Hildita would visit. He would play with the children and his Alsatian, or they would watch football or boxing on the TV together—though his favorite form of relaxation was doing mathematics or playing chess. With the children, as with his men, he was a stern disciplinarian, smacking them and refusing to let the nanny comfort them so they would remember what they had been punished for.

'Sometimes we revolutionaries are alone, even our children see us as strangers,' he wrote.

He was equally strict at the ministry. If someone had had an affair with another man's wife, covered up a mistake, or got a relative a job, they would be hauled in front of Che, who would offer the miscreant a chance to expunge their misdemeanor by a 'voluntary' stretch in Guanahacabibes labor camps. And peasants from his old column in the Sierra were confined to a collective farm where they were forced to do schoolwork. Che would check up on them regularly and was harsh with those who did not make progress.

'Che had something of the missionary about him,' said a colleague.

Aleida was forced to give back a pair of Italian shoes given to her by Celia Sánchez, Fidel's lover—on the grounds that no ordinary Cuban could afford imported shoes. He was livid when he found that his family had been given a food supplement and insisted on having the same rations as everyone else. And when one of the children was sick, he refused Aleida permission to use the car to take the child to hospital. She should take the bus like everyone else.

Even though Aleida was now putting on weight too, Che was still powerfully attracted to her. He would read the love poetry of Pablo Neruda to her in the bedroom at night and when his mother-in-law in Santa Clara asked him once whether he wanted a bath he said: 'Not if Aleida is not in it.' On the other hand, Aleida knew that what Che really needed was mothering. She would feed him, bathe him, and dress him.

Socially, Che was an oddball in Cuba, where people loved parties, music, and rum—instead he was solitary, drank red wine when he could get it, and had no time for music. Cubans liked to relax on the beach. Che could not swim. They ate pork; he ate beef. They slugged back little shots of coffee; he sucked maté. Their humor was coarse and bawdy; his sly and ironic. They were relaxed, while he was stern and rigid, considered overly serious, moralistic, and holier-than-thou by many.

And although he considered himself above all a Latin American, everyone around him thought of him as an Argentinian. He just did not fit in. However, he gathered around him a number of fanatical followers who were known as *los hombres del Che*.

The only thing he did that was typically Cuban was smoke cigars. This was disastrous for his asthma. Indeed the humid climate of the island was bad for his lungs. Cuba has one of the highest rates of asthma and it was probably the worst place in the world for him to live.

What Cubans really could not understand about him was that he seemed to be totally faithful to his wife—this was in a country where most men had two or three mistresses tucked away. Women flocked to him. When one flirted with him openly at a reception, he told her to behave herself. But he was not inured. When sat next to the beautiful daughter of an ambassador, he had to excuse himself, saying that he could not bear it anymore. In that case, he was asked, how had he got married to someone as ugly as Hilda. He replied that she was a good comrade—besides you did not have to be good looking to be good in bed. Later he admitted that he had had rather too many drinks when he agreed to marry her.

In fact, Che was not as faithful as he made out. Although he condemned adultery in others, he acknowledged paternity of Omar Pérez, born in 1964, son of Lilia Rosa Pérez who he met in Santa Clara in 1958.

Then an attractive woman in her thirties, Lilia Rosa Pérez met Che in Santa Clara in 1958, then again in La Cabaña in 1959. The affair continued for some years as, on March 19, 1964, she gave birth to his son in Havana. The child was named Omar after Omar Khayyam—Che had given his mother a copy of the *Rubaiyat*.

The boy grew up to be a poet too, but a dissident. For opposing Castro and refusing to do military service, he found himself in one of the labor camps his father had established.

In the late 1980s, Lilia introduced Omar to Che's daughter Hildita, who had been sidelined by her father's official widow and children. By then, she was an alcoholic, stricken by cancer and depression. Both out of favor with the regime they found solace in their kinship.

Another of Che's illegitimate children, Mirko, also found himself at odds with the government.

Che particularly did not like being treated as a celebrity. When he crashed into the back of a car on the Malecón, the driver told him that he would not have the coachwork fixed, so proud was he to have a dent inflicted by Che. This was an embarrassment. And when a soldier brought Che his boots, freshly shined, he called the man a *guataca*—'brownnoser'—and kicked his ass. Then man then flung the boots in the street and Che docked his pay for a week.

In March 1963, Che addressed a meeting of Argentinians in Havana, concerning the need for revolution in his homeland and calling for support from the Perónists. This antagonized the Communists who had turned against the armed struggle. Then in July, the Argentine military allowed elections to be held. Nevertheless, Che sent a guerrilla vanguard who established a base in Bolivia and began armed incursions over the border.

'You go and set up a group and have them wait for me,' he told them, 'I will come soon.'

Seeking new allies, Che himself attended the first-anniversary celebrations for Algerian independence. Soon after a Cuban armored battalion fought for Algeria in its war against neighboring Morocco.

While the Cuban economy now depended totally on the support Castro had obtained from the Soviet Union, Che turned against Moscow and began taking a pro-Beijing line. Indeed Che's ministry was the only one to employ Chinese advisers. Unlike the Soviet ones, they asked for no salary or preferential housing and, in Che's eyes, were closer to the Socialist 'new man.' The Soviets were also afraid that the guerrilla adventures in Latin America would provoke another confrontation with the US, while Krushchev was still pursuing his policy of 'peaceful co-existence,' which annoyed Che. The Argentine Communists even branded Guevara a Trotskyite. A party was sent from the Presidium of the Supreme Soviet to investigate. Che explained to deputy party secretary Nikolai Metutsov that he was not a Maoist and that he was a 'true friend of the Soviet Union and the Leninist Party.' While he spoke Metutsov admitted falling in love with him. He told Che: 'I am a little older than you, but I like you, I like your looks.' Then he confessed to Che his love for him because 'he was a very attractive man.'

Plainly Metutsov was besotted.

'He had very beautiful eyes," Metutsov said. 'Magnificent eyes, so deep, so generous, so honest, a stare that was so honest that somehow, one could not help feel it… and he spoke very well, he became inwardly excited, and his speech was like that, with all of this impetus, as if his words were squeezing you… In our conversations I had the impression that he knew his portrait already hung on history's walls, the history of the national liberation movement. He was sufficiently intelligent to understand this, without arrogance, while remaining a normal person.'

Metutsov concluded that while Che had been contaminated by Maoist slogans—believing, like Mao that all 'political power grows out of the barrel of a gun'—and like Trotsky, he had sought to foment revolution in Latin America, he was, deep down, a Marxist-Leninist. However, it was plain that, for Che, peaceful co-existence was an anathema. Although he admitted that, though nobody says it, the Western bloc is advancing faster than the people's democracies , he believed that this was because the Soviet bloc had abandoned the path of Marxist-Leninism, rather than adhered to it.

Meanwhile Castro was going behind everyone's back and trying to patch up a behind-scenes-détente with President Kennedy when Kennedy was assassinated in Dallas on November 22, 1963. Che was a suspect at the time.

Many of those suspected to have been involved in the assassination and the murder of Lee Harvey Oswald—Kennedy's alleged assassin—had Cuban connections. One FBI agent even reported seeing Che with Jack Ruby—the man who shot Oswald—in Panama.

Castro continued making overtures to Kennedy's successor, Lyndon Johnson. Che spoke out against this, telling the Cubans that it was their common duty to fight imperialism 'wherever it appears and with all the weapons at our disposal.' Of this growing split with Castro, Che said: 'With Fidel, I want neither marriage nor divorce.' Che was now so marginalized that the price the CIA put on his head fell to $20,000, while Castro was still worth $100,000.

While Che was in Europe to speak at the founding of the UN Conference on Trade and Development in spring 1964, he learnt that his guerrilla vanguard in Argentina had been captured and destroyed. Their money, weapons and personnel had been traced back to him. Back in Havana Alberto Granado remarked that Che had 'the face of a dead dog.'

'You see me here, behind a desk, fucked,' he replied, 'while my people die during missions I've sent them on.'

He was also disillusioned with the Kremlin line. Support from Moscow—or even Beijing—was imperialism with another name. What Cuba needed was support from other, like-minded states in Latin America. And he resolved to leave Cuba and return to the battlefield.

Long ago, he had concluded: 'It is worth dying on a foreign beach for such a noble ideal.'

Chapter Eight—An African Adventure, 1965

With the Cuban Revolution now secure, Guevara decided that it was time to leave and create new revolutions elsewhere. It should not have been too hard to find a spot.

'Revolution,' said Che, 'can be made at any given moment anywhere in the world.'

However, his guerrilla vanguard in Argentina had failed, causing some to doubt his self-generating *foco* theory. Arms were sent to the new Tupamaro guerrilla group in Uruguay and Tania was sent to Bolivia to discover the fate of any survivors from the Argentine fiasco and assess the possibilities for revolution there.

Meanwhile Che tried to find a role in international diplomacy. He visited the new regime in the Soviet Union after the fall of Krushchev, then went to Beijing in a misguided attempt to patch things up between Russia and China. Then in December 1964, Che went to New York as head of the Cuban delegation to the United Nations General Assembly.

In a television interview, he was so charming that his assured performance drew protests from other Latin American countries. But in front of the General Assembly, he was a firebrand, saying that while 'peaceful coexistence' might exist between sovereign states, as a Marxist, he maintained that it could not exist 'between exploiters and the exploited, between the oppressors and the oppressed.' He then turned his attention to the situation in the Congo, condemning 'Western imperialism' there and saying: 'All the free men in the world must stand ready to avenge the crime of the Congo.'

*

The situation in post-colonial Congo was dire. In June 1960, Congo had won its independence from Belgium under the leadership of Prime Minister Patrice Lumumba (1923–61). Within weeks elements of the army had rebelled and the mineral-rich region of Katanga had seceded. On the pretext of defending Belgian citizens, Belgium troops landed and lent their support to the breakaway regime of Moise Tshombe. Lumumba called for UN intervention, but when UN troops failed to expel the Belgians, he turned for help to the Soviet Union.

In September Lumumba was dismissed by President Joseph Kasavubu. With CIA backing the head of the army Colonel Joseph Mobutu (1930–1997) staged a coup during which Lumumba was handed over to the Katangese separatists and killed. Then in February 1961, Mobutu handed power back to President Kasavubu, staying on as commander in chief of the army. In the summer of 1964, Lumumba's supporters rallied under former minister of education Pierre Mulele, who had Chinese backing and seized Stanleyville, now Kisangani, in the northeast of the country. They took hostage the American consul, scores of US missionaries and three hundred Belgian citizens and, reportedly, killed 20,000 wealthy Congolese. The US sent paratroopers, while the Congolese government employed white mercenaries from Rhodesia— now Zimbabwe—and South Africa, commanded by British mercenary 'Mad' Mike Hoare.

In 1965, Mobutu staged another coup, this time holding on to the presidency himself. He ruled by decree and the Movement for the

Revolution, which he headed, became the only party permitted. He nationalized the copper mines in Katanga and Africanised names throughout the country. In October 1971, he changed the nation's name to the Republic of Zaire. The following January he took the name Mobutu Sese Seko Koko Ngbendu Wa Za Banga—which means 'the all-powerful warrior who, because of his endurance and inflexible will to win, will go from conquest to conquest, leaving a wake of fire'. He looted the country, amassing one of the world's largest fortunes abroad and destroying the infrastructure of the country in the process. With the end of the Cold War, Mobutu lost Western support for his government, but he managed to hold onto power until, in 1997, friendless and ill, he was ousted by rebel leader Laurent Kabila and went into exile.

Kabila was assassinated in 2001 and succeeded by his son Joseph, who had maintained power after a series of challenged elections, while in the east reaches of the country the warfare continues.

*

Guevara had been studying the situation in the Congo for some time. The Lumumbists, he believed, were involved in an anti-imperialist struggle and conditions existed for revolution there that could not be found in Latin America. The rebels enjoyed popular support. There were a number of countries in the region who would help. As the Congo was not in the US's Latin American back yard, the Soviets would not oppose his intervention there. He also saw the Congo as the Bolivia of Africa, surrounded by other countries that were vulnerable to revolution. And he believed that if he was successful there, the Soviets might change their mind and back the struggle in Latin America.

In his speech to the UN, he condemned the organization itself for being a tool of 'white imperialism' in Africa and for excluding Communist China in favor of US-backed Nationalist government of Chiang Kai-shek confined to the island of Taiwan. (The People's Republic of China took over the Republic of China's seat on the Security Council in 1971.) The US was, of course, singled out for criticism. How could it pretend to defend the interests of black people in Africa, when black people within the US itself were being oppressed.

His speech made him few friends. The US ambassador to the US and several Latin America envoys protested. Exiled Cubans held a noisy protest outside. A number of *gusanos* were arrested after firing a bazooka at the UN building from across the East River and a woman tried to stab Che in the lobby.

While in the US, Guevara spoke with Democrat Senator Eugene McCarthy, who would become a leading opponent of the Vietnam war. During the interview Che boasted openly of Cuba's revolutionary activities in Latin America. At the very time Castro was making overtures to the US once again, Guevara was promising the imperialists' 'extermination.' However, Che did not take the opportunity to visit Malcolm X—even though his help had been sought to recruit black Americans to fight in Africa—fearing that if they shared the same platform it might be construed as interfering in the internal affairs of the United States.

Journalists and diplomats alike were soon remarking that Che would shortly be leaving Cuba. His departure was not entirely voluntary. In a speech in Algiers, he accused the Soviet Union of profiteering from its trade with Cuba and being 'an accomplice with imperialism.' Moscow began to reconsider its support for Cuba and when Che returned to Havana he went into long, secret talks with Fidel and Raúl Castro, who had come down on the side of Moscow in the Sino-Soviet split. Raúl accused Guevara of being pro-Chinese and a Trotskyist—which Che, a life-long Stalinist, violently rejected. But it was clear that there was no role left in Cuba for Guevara. As a result it was decided that Che should head the Cuba military mission to the Congo. He resigned from his position in the government, gave up his Cuban citizenship, and left the country in disguise as bespectacled, clean-shaven business man Ramón Benítez.

He left Aleida a tape of him reciting her favorite love poems and a letter to be read to his children in the event of his death. In fact, his marriage was already in trouble. He told Nasser: 'I already have two broken marriages.'

He had been away once again when Aleida gave birth to his son Ernesto on February 24, 1965. Hilda and Hildita were not told of the Congo expedition. They were simply told that he was going to cut sugar cane in the countryside and would contact them when he got back. This cover story was spread widely. Che's mother was also told that he was cane-cutting as penance for having spoken out in Algeria. It also seems that he left without saying goodbye to Castro.

In the letter to his children he wrote: 'If one day you must read this letter, it will be because I am no longer among you. You will almost not remember me and the littlest ones will remember nothing at all. Your father has been a man who acted according to his beliefs and has been faithful to his convictions. Grow up good revolutionaries... Remember that the Revolution is what is important and that each one of us, on their own, is worthless. Above all, try always to be able to feel deeply any injustice committed against any person in any part of the world. It is the most beautiful quality of a revolutionary. Until always, little children, I still hope to see you again. A really big kiss and a hug from Papa.'

Elsewhere, he said: 'Let me say, with the risk of appearing ridiculous, that the true revolutionary is guided by strong feelings of love. It is impossible to think of an authentic revolutionary without this quality. This is perhaps one of the greatest dramas of a leader; he must combine an impassioned spirit with a cold mind and make painful decisions without flinching a muscle. Our vanguard revolutionaries must idealize their love for the people, for the most sacred causes, and make it one and indivisible. They cannot descend, with small doses of daily affection, to the places where ordinary men put their love into practice. The leaders of the Revolution have children who do not learn to call their father with their first faltering words. They have wives who must be part of the general sacrifice of their lives to carry the Revolution to its destiny. Their friends are strictly limited to their comrades in revolution. There is no life outside it.'

In April 1965, Che arrived at the base of the Congo's Soviet-backed Committee for National Liberation on the border of neighboring Rwanda and Burundi. By that time the insurrection within the Congo had been put down in a bloodbath that involved the murder of around eighty Western hostages and the massacre of thousands of Congolese by white mercenaries.

Che's intention was to cultivate the French-educated Laurent Kabila, then in his mid-twenties and one of a number of the Congo's rebel leaders. Guevara was distressed to find that most African countries boasted a number of rival rebel groups, whose leaders lived on Communist handouts in Dar es Salaam.

'The scotch and the women are also covered by friendly governments and if one likes good scotch and beautiful women, that costs a lot of money,' he wrote.

But these would-be revolutionaries were only concerned with the situation in their own countries. They did not see, as Che did, that Africans faced a single continent-wide struggle against a common enemy—the United States. Having put aside his plans to be a new San Martín or Simón Bolívar, sweeping through Latin America country by country, he now envisioned a tri-continental struggle against the US.

In Angola, the Cubans backed the MPLA, who faced a two-decade struggle against the Portuguese colonialists and Jonas Samibi's rival UNITA. In the Congo, Che backed Kabila because he shared his anti-American views—even though Kabila had lied to him when they first met. He claimed that he had just returned from fighting in the interior when, in fact, he had been spending his time in the bars and brothels of the resort town of Kigoma on the Tanzanian shore of Lake Tanganyika.

Che had not even been invited to join the struggle in the Congo. He had imposed himself on it. As it was, the official head of the military mission was Víctor Dreke, a black Cuban, and although Nasser had warned Che not to play Tarzan—a white man leading and protecting the blacks—this is exactly what he proceeded to do. Indeed most of the 130 Cubans who fought in the Congo were black. Che regretted this as he considered them less academically or politically developed. He arrived using a code name *Tatu*, Swahili for 'three.' No one had been told that he was coming as he believed that, once he was there, it would be difficult for them to turn him away. He had already burned his bridges.

The situation Che found was hopeless. Kabila found excuses to stay away from the front. The other commanders spent their time in the fleshpots of Kigoma, while the men in the field depended for their protection on *dawa*—a magic potion which they thought made them invulnerable to bullets, unless they showed fear, stole, or touched a woman. Che was not about to find the 'new man' in Africa.

Che finally revealed who he was to the rebel's political commissar. But fearing an international scandal, he insisted 'no one must find out, please, no one must find out'. But the man then scooted off to Dar es Salaam to inform Kabila.

As it was the guerrillas' numbers were depleted more by venereal disease than by battle casualties and Che was concerned that the revolution's money was being spent on prostitutes. He also had to treat alcohol poisoning caused by the local *pombe*, a lethal brew distilled from maize and manioc flour. And there were accidental gunshot wounds.

'Since scarcely anyone had the faintest idea about guns, they tended to go off when they were played with or treated without care,' wrote Che.

He proposed training a column of guerrillas. While they were out in the field, he would train a second column and send them out when the first returned. That way he hoped to develop a revolutionary cadre. But he was met with prevarication. The best he could do was organize classes in French, Swahili, and 'general culture.'

When local people heard that there was a doctor with the guerrillas, they flocked to the dispensary for treatment. Other rebel groups turned up to pillage the huge quantities of Chinese and Soviet medicines, weapons, and ammunition that were being dumped on the beach by the Tanzanians, claiming 'fantastic totals for the number of men in the groups.' Soon the Cubans began coming down with tropical disease, weakness, apathy and pessimism.

Che moved to a camp 8,000 feet up in the mountains, where his men were joined by Tutsis who had fled Rwanda after independence when the Hutus had begun slaughtering them. However, the Rwandans and the Congolese did not get on. Che came down with a fever and was just recovering when orders came to attack the enemy stronghold at Albertville, a mining town 125 miles to the south. He only had thirty men, ten of whom were ill. But Che prepared for battle anyway. Then seventeen fresh Cubans turned up, reporting that more were on their way. But they brought bad news. Che's mother Celia was terminally ill. In fact, she died three days before this message had arrived as attempts to contact him proved fruitless as the family still believed he was in Cuba.

In her last letter to her beloved Ernesto, his mother wrote: 'My dear one,... It seems to me true madness that, with so few heads in Cuba with the ability to organize, you should all go and cut cane for a month... when there are so many good cane cutters among the people... And this is not a mother speaking. It's an old woman who hopes to see the whole world converted to socialism. I believe that if you go through with this, you will not be giving your best service to the cause of world socialism. If all roads in Cuba have been closed to you, for whatever reason, in Algiers there's a Mr Ben Bella who would appreciate your organizing his economy, or advising him on it; or a Mr Nkrumah in Ghana who would welcome the same help. Yes, you'll always be a foreigner. That seems to be your permanent fate.'

Che managed to persuade the Congolese commander Laurent Mitoudidi that an attack on Albertville was premature. Guerrillas were sent out to assess the situation. They reported back that most of the field commanders spent their time getting drunk, while their men mistreated the peasants who were forced to bring them food.

'The basic feature of the People's Liberation Army was that it was a parasitic army,' Che wrote. 'It did not work, did not train, did not fight and demanded provisions and labor from the population, sometimes with extreme harshness.'

Even the Congolese under his command refused to carry any more than their basic equipment, saying: 'I am not a truck' and later 'I am not a Cuban.'

Mitoudidi did his best to whip his men into shape, punishing persistent *pombe* drinkers and giving heavy weapons only to those who could use them. However, he could not commit his men to action without Kabila's approval. And Kabila still had not turned up. Soon after Mitoudidi fell into the waters of Lake Tanganyika. The men on the boat he had been traveling on cut the engine and could not start it again because of some mysterious magnetic force, they said. Apparently, the lake was inhabited by all manner of evil spirits and they could not maneuver back to the spot where Mitoudidi drowned fifteen minutes later. Che wrote about this incident in his *African Diary* in a chapter called 'A Hope Dies.' Morale among the Cubans was not helped when they asked for boots and vitamins, and Che replied that the Africans went barefoot and had no access to medicines.

Orders then came to attack the garrison at Bendera where three hundred enemy soldiers and a hundred mercenaries were well dug in. Che struck with a force of forty Cubans and 160 Congolese and Rwandans. It was a disaster. A third of the Congolese deserted before the fighting started. Others simply refused to fight. Many of the Tutsis fled leaving their weapons and four of the Cubans were killed. Their bodies were discovered on the battlefield by Mike Hoare's mercenaries and the news that Cubans were fighting in Africa went out on the wire services. The CIA station chief in the Congo began to suspect that they were being led by Guevara, but failed to convince Langley. However, they did send anti-Castro Cubans to fight, though the two groups never confronted each other.

Che's spirits revived when more Cuban veterans turned up, led by Harry Villegas. But he warned them that they risked death at the hands of their African comrades who could shoot properly. News came through that Castro had published the letter in which Che renounced his Cuban citizenship. This estranged him from his men. He consoled himself, as usual, with reading. Other Cubans became so dispirited that he had to let some of them go home, then he heard that Algerian President Ben Bella, who had been backing the expedition, had been removed in a coup. Kabila turned up, but left after five days to organize more aid. His presence raised morale, but afterwards the rebels turned on each other. One commander shot his deputy for producing bad *dawa* at Bendera.

The Cubans staged a number of successful raids, but the Congolese and Rwandans ran away. On August 12, Che wrote a note to his Cubans, saying: 'A war is not won with such troops.' Then the Cuban rearguard wrote suggesting that they send men to set up a guerrilla training camp to train Mozambicans and other African revolutionaries; Che advised against it, warning of the 'indiscipline, disorganization and complete demoralization' they would find.

Che proposed overhauling the command system, instituting a training program and sending men out to seize the arms of deserters. But he was refused to go out in the field to instigate any of this. At the time, there was a power struggle going on within the Congolese ranks with some leaders negotiating with the enemy and field commanders refused to send their men to be trained. The rebels managed to mount some ambushes under the command of Cuban instructors. But the Tanzanians sided with the Congolese who were negotiating and halted the flow of supplies. Che tried to rally the African troops, without success. Those returning from training in Bulgaria and Romania wanted leave to see their families. Instead Che proposed recruiting and training a peasant army from scratch. Unfortunately, a careless Cuban managed to set the village selected as a training camp on fire. Somehow, from amid the exploding bullets and grenades, Che's diary was saved. Nevertheless, Guevara was bullish. He wrote to Fidel, saying 'in the name of proletarian internationalism... I can assure you that, were it not for me, this beautiful dream would have collapsed into general chaos long ago.'

Again he tried to rally his own men to save the cause of the Congolese, but then, like many of his men, he was struck down with gastro-enteritis on top of endemic malaria.

'Until the rigors of the job got the better of my scientific spirit', he wrote, 'I noted in my field diary the statistics of my own case: I had the runs more than thirty times in twenty-four hours. Only the scrub knows how many more there were after that.'

During his time in the Congo, Che lost a quarter of his body weight. But the suffering of Che and his men was wasted. The Congolese refused to obey his orders and when he told them off—in French which was then translated into Swahili—they simply laughed. And despite his ideological objections he hired a witchdoctor of his own to help control the African fighters.

Che found himself holding the line while the other parties to the conflict were busy making peace. A deal was being brokered that the white mercenaries supporting the government would be expelled, provided the Cubans left as well. There was to be no foreign intervention on either side. At the same time, on October 24—exactly six months after he had entered the Congo—his base camp was overrun. He had had time to set fire to the huts, but a lot of material was needlessly lost, along with Che's two pet monkeys. He had not posted sentries and his men had fled at the sight—not of the vanguard of the enemy force—but of the peasants fleeing before them. Che blamed himself. Even his own men began disobeying his orders. Instead of waiting on a hillside as they had been told, a group of them had made off. Now there were just thirteen left. Che reflected that was just one more than Fidel had had after the *Granma* landing, 'but I am not the same leader,' he said.

Ahead of them they found abandoned villages and mud—it was now the rainy season. Refugees berated them, saying that the government troops had carried off their wives and there was nothing they could do about it as the rebels had not given them any guns. A wounded Cuban who they had been carrying died. It was their sixth fatality, but the first time they had had a body to bury.

'It was a mute and virile accusation against my stupidity and lack of foresight,' wrote Che, 'as had been his conduct from the moment he received the wound.'

The Congolese rebel leaders began to blame the deteriorating military situation on the Cubans, accusing them of being cowardly and treacherous. More of them began to respond to peace feelers put out by the government. Che was warned that he risked being cut off from his lakeside camp and, eventually, withdrew to the lake.

Although the Rwandans and Congolese were deserting en masse, Che was determined to fight on with twenty hand-picked men, or make a thousand-mile hike across the Congolese jungle to where Mulele was still fighting in the west. A peace settlement, backed by the Soviet Union, had been agreed in Accra and the Tanzanian government withdrew its support, even patrolling the lake with gunboats to prevent further supplies getting through. But Che planned a breakout to the south in an attempt to get behind the on-coming government forces and disrupt their supply lines. But the operation seemed futile without the support of the locals. Even one of his own men told him to stop 'running over the hills without these people's cooperation.'

Che's officers decided unanimously to leave the battlefield. They had lost faith in the revolution. Even if the rebels won, they said, they did not have men of principle as leaders who would push through the social advances that had been made in Cuba. Che, conscious of his place in history, then tried to get something in writing from the Congolese, saying that it was a Congolese decision to end the fighting, not a Cuban one. But this was now academic as even the base camp dissolved in chaos.

They radioed for boats to come and evacuate them, then marched down the lakeside to the rendezvous point. The boats took two days to arrive. During that time Che wracked his brain to find a way to stay on. But the situation was hopeless. Even the Congolese had turned against them. When the boats turned up there were not enough of them to carry all the rebels. Che had to trick some of them into staying behind. Machine guns were trained on them from the boats in case they caused trouble. But they did nothing, except sob, knowing they had been abandoned to their fate. Che said he never felt more alone.

But he was not as alone as he thought. No-one has satisfactorily explained how the Cubans managed to escape across Lake Tanganyika which was patrolled by boats and planes manned by mercenaries, government troops, the Belgians, anti-Castro Cubans, and the CIA. And it was as well that they did not run into any trouble. Che had ordered 75mm recoilless rifles to be mounted in the prow of the boats. If they had been fired, the after-blast would have killed all those on board.

Chapter Nine—Death in Bolivia, 1965-1967

The ill and emaciated Guevara spent several weeks recovering in a small bedroom and office that had been set up for him on the first floor of the Cuban embassy in Dar es Salaam, wondering what to do next. The publication of his letter renouncing his Cuban citizenship made it impossible to live there again. His economic reforms had been overturned. Workers were now being offered material incentives which helped revive the economy. Castro was as steadfastly pro-Soviet as ever and had even reached a slight rapprochement with America, having negotiated US entry visas for any Cuban wishing to leave the island.

Che's first thought was to return to Argentina to start a revolution there. Castro did everything in his power to prevent this as he was convinced that Guevara would be killed by the Argentine gendarmerie. He even sent Aleida to Tanzania to see him. They stayed in his rooms for six weeks with the curtains drawn. He would send her a list of books to read which they discussed at the end of each day. It was the closest thing they ever had to a honeymoon, she said.

After writing up his notes from the fighting in the Congo, Che agreed to go to Prague. Ill and depressed, he spent four months in Czechoslovakia. Aleida visited again and Castro sent other people in an attempt to persuade Che not to go to Argentina. One of them was Tania who had seen action in Bolivia. She was the lover of Che's bodyguard who Che summarily dismissed on the grounds that, as a black man, he stood out. There were rumors of an affair.

Castro also approached various guerrilla groups in Venezuela and Peru to see if they would not take Che. But the rivalry between Communists and Fidelístas in Latin America made this a problem. However, the Cubans had maintained good relations with the Communists in Bolivia and the secretary-general of the Bolivian Communist Party Mario Monje agreed to accept Che, provided that he was using Bolivia as a base for starting a revolution in Argentina, rather than trying to foment one in Bolivia itself. Indeed, Che had told Monje at a meeting in Havana in 1964 that the conditions were not right for revolution in Bolivia. Land reform meant that the Indians would not support a guerrilla struggle. Castro promised that this was the case. However, Che planned another guerrilla movement in Bolivia which would spread revolution to the surrounding countries until the whole of Latin America was Communist. It was at least as ambitious as anything the conquistadors had planned.

Che now consented to return to Cuba, where he recuperated in the rest home in eastern Havana, where his presence was known only to a few, and made preparations for his new expedition. He handpicked a squad of twenty comrades from the Sierra Maestra, the Congo, his bodyguard and the Ministry of Industries. They did not know where they were going to fight or who their commander would be until a balding, middle-aged man named Ramón, turned up at the camp and started insulting them. It was only when some of them took offence, that Ramón revealed himself to be Che in disguise. Then training began in earnest. Woken at five, they would start shooting practice at six. At eleven they would have an hour's rest before an eight-mile forced march over hilly terrain carrying a ten-pound rucksack. After another hour's rest they would be given classes in mathematics, history and languages, finishing off with a two-hour class in Quechua, the indigenous language of Bolivia. At weekends they would get pep talks from Castro and other high officials. Che also completed a scathing critique of *Economía Política*, the Stalin-era manual on the construction of a socialist economy. In it he laid the failure of the Soviet regime at Lenin's door and predicted that Russia would return to capitalism. It has never been published.

Tania returned to La Paz, where she had married, and hid the Cubans as they were infiltrated. Meanwhile Bolivians were sent to Cuba for training. The Bolivian Communists grew suspicious when Che's top lieutenants arrived. Then the French Marxist writer Régis Debray, a close confident of Castro's, turned up to make contact with Maoist groups, and the Bolivian Communist Party realized that Che was not just going to be passing through but was aiming to establish a guerrilla *foco* in Bolivia itself. Monje reacted by trying to persuade the Cubans to base their activities not in the northwest of the country, where conditions were favorable, but in the deserted southeast. Che was not privy to this faction fighting and considered that the southeast was better for his own individual purposes as it was closer to Argentina.

The twenty-one guerrilla fighters were supplied with false biographies. Che posed as a Uruguayan, others as Peruvians or Bolivians. He tried to keep their departure secret and only allowed the other men to say goodbye to their families after Aleida had turned up at the camp. He met his children, but only in his disguise as Uncle 'Ramón.' And until the very last moment, Castro tried to persuade him not to go. They stayed up all night talking. But Che was determined to go ahead, even though it was clear that Monje was obstructing their plans. The two comrades parted with a manly hug. Castro was seen later with his head hung low. His men wondered whether he had been crying.

Che arrived in Bolivia in November 1966 to find that Monje had not provided the twenty guerrillas he had promised and that the Maoists shunned him. Instead he tried to recruit his own local force. In the camp at Ñancahuazú in the south of the country, he found no food, no medicine, few weapons, and telecommunication equipment that was practically useless. Worse, he was up against a formidable enemy. Since the agreement signed with Milton Eisenhower in 1953, Bolivia had become a more or less stable democracy, supported by US military aid in quantities second only to that America supplied Israel. Over a thousand Bolivian Officers had been to the School of the Americas in Panama, the US's notorious 'coup school' that taught counterinsurgency by fair means or foul. Even so, army was popular among the peasants because they built roads and schools in rural areas and the president, an army officer, spoke fluent Quechua. This was not a banana republic and a down-trodden indigenous population just waiting to be liberated. The mineral resources had been nationalized and were exploited by radical labor unions.

Tania brought Monje, who had been out of the country, to Che's headquarters in December 1966. Che began by admitting that the Cubans had lied. Bolivia was going to be the centre of their revolutionary activities, not Argentina. Monje said that he would only join them if the military command came under his political leadership. Bolivians must be in charge. Che refused as being forced to submit to others' authority had tied his hands in Africa. Castro tried to broker an agreement with other Bolivian Communists in Havana, trying to persuade them that he should be in charge because the aim was to foment revolution throughout Latin America. However, there was no guerrilla activity in nearby Peru or Argentina, and never any possibility of any in Brazil—and the Bolivians did not even give Che the logistical support they had promised. But it did not matter to Che that he did not have the support of the people in Bolivia, or anywhere else. He was a conquistador and would take over by force.

Discipline was poor. The supply officer spent much of his time seducing local women. Nevertheless Che set out on a reconnaissance mission. The terrain they encountered was much worse than anything in the Sierra Maestra. The vegetation was so thick they had to cut through it with machetes. They were supposed to be out for a fortnight. Lost in the jungle, they were away forty-eight days. They were plagued with mosquitoes and the boro fly, which laid its eggs under the skin. There was little game to hunt. They were reduced to eating monkeys, parrots, and palm hearts. The rain was torrential and three men were drowned crossing mountain streams and weapons were lost. Che returned after four weeks, emaciated and with swollen hands and feet, to discover that his headquarters had been discovered by the army.

Two Bolivian new recruits who had deserted were captured by the Bolivian army. They confirmed other reports by peasants that guerrillas were operating in the area. Another Bolivian had even boasted to an oil man of the guerrillas' prowess. Knowing that Guevara was in the area, the army had sent a patrol to investigate the ranch house at Ñancahuazú. The guard surrendered without a fight though, in a skirmish that followed, a soldier was killed. The army was certain to be back.

Although Che's force was in no way ready for combat, he prepared for a fight.

Three days later, aircraft alerted the guerrilla force to the army's advance. His men executed a perfect ambush. Seven of the army unit were killed, including one officer. Another fourteen surrendered, four of whom were wounded. The guerrillas took two Uzis, one machine gun, three mortars, sixteen rifles, and two thousand rounds of ammunition for the loss of not a single casualty. It seemed that Che had not lost his touch.

The Bolivian government responded by banning the Communist Party, preventing an uprising in the cities which might have helped Che's guerrillas. It also prevented Tania and Régis Debray, who had now turned up, returning to La Paz. Vital information identifying her had been left behind and Che slapped her when he found her in his camp dressed in combat fatigues. But she was infatuated by Che and would go to any length to be by his side.

Their transmitters broke down, leaving them cut off from the outside world, and there were more desertions. These led to the Bolivian army overrunning the guerrillas' camp on April 7. However, three days later, the army were lured into an ambush. Then the guerrillas feinted and attacked again, leaving nine soldiers dead, twelve wounded and thirteen captured. Che's men had suffered only one casualty and made another significant haul of weapons and ammunition. The Bolivian army were now claiming that they were up against a force of five hundred highly trained guerrillas and the Bolivian president visited the area. Inevitably the US took a hand. They sent twenty Green Berets and two Cuban CIA men who began a nineteen-week course for several hundred Bolivian troops destined to become the country's first Rangers.

Although they knew he was there, neither the Bolivian nor the US authorities disclosed that it was Che Guevara they were looking for, in case the presence of the legendary guerrilla fighter sparked other uprisings in the area. While Che was on the run, *Tricontinental* magazine in Havana published an essay in which he called for 'the creation of two, three, many Vietnams.' In it he also extolled 'unbending hatred for the enemy, which pushes the human being beyond his natural limitations, making him into an effective, violent, selective and cold-blooding killing machine… people without hatred cannot triumph over a brutal enemy.' He hoped to start a world war where Socialism would emerge triumphant. The spirit of the conquistador was not limited to Latin America. He wanted to take over the whole world.

In the hope of building international support, Che sought to arrange the safe departure of Régis Debray and Che's Argentine lieutenant, the painter Ciros Bustos, who aimed to aid the revolution in Argentina. To do that, he split his force, taking the two men south toward the town of Muyupampa, which he aimed to attack in the hope that the two men could escape in the ensuing confusion. However, the army had already reached Muyupampa and the guerrillas were met by Anglo-Chilean journalist George Andrew Roth, who said he had been led to them by some children. Roth agreed to vouch for the status of Debray and Bustos as journalists. This did not work. They two men were arrested, but saved from summary execution when a local newspaper photographer took their picture. When the photography was published, world opinion, and the CIA intervened. They were sentenced to thirty years, but were released after three when a new government came to power.

Meanwhile Che had lost contact with his rearguard and with no radio equipment, they never reestablished contact—though more than once they came within a few hundred yards and even opened fire on each other. Tania was with the other group. Che persisted searching for them, even though his men begged him to give up and he never saw her again.

Che sought to build support for the guerrillas among the peasants, but the death of two civilians turned them against him—even though he worked as a dentist for them. When forced, they would sell him supplies, but immediately inform the authorities of the contact. Soon thousands of soldiers were combing the area for forty weak and hungry men.

Che's men occupied villages, staged ambushes, and performed defensive maneuvers but, in Guevara's time in Bolivia, he never went on the attack. According to some accounts, the guerrillas were even doing quite well, but Che was cut off from the cities and losing men. Without reinforcements his campaign was doomed.

By this time Che was ill. On 16 May, he wrote: 'As soon as we started walking, I was hit by a terrible colic and diarrhea. They stopped it with Demarol and I lost consciousness while they carried me in a hammock. When I woke up, I felt much relieved, but I was runny all over like an unweaned baby… I stank to high heaven.'

His asthma returned. With no drugs to control it, he tried various homemade potions, smoking various herbs, and hanging from a branch while his men beat his chest with rifle butts. He could no longer carry a rucksack and, when he became unable to walk, he rode on a mule. The others were killed and eaten. On June 14, his thirty-ninth birthday, he wrote: 'The time is inexorably approaching when I must reconsider my future as a guerrilla. For now, I am still in one piece.'

His determination never flagged. He told his men that they were fortunate that they had been given the 'opportunity to become revolutionaries, the highest step in the human ladder, and also allows us to test ourselves.' But his weakened condition had begun to affect his judgment. While Che hid, his men occupied the town of Samaipata, but they found no medicine. But then, instead of heading on into Chapare where the terrain was better suited for guerrilla warfare, they returned south. Monje realized that Che was now doomed. He headed for Havana where he intended to present a plan for Che's escape. But he traveled via Chile. The Chilean Communists were not sympathetic. The Cubans refused a visa and he was delayed in Santiago until after Che was dead. Castro had planned to reinforce the expedition but Soviet premier Alexei Kosygin who arrived in Havana on July 26, after a visit to the US, told him to stop provoking the Americans and persuaded him to leave Che to his own devices.

Equipment left buried in a cave was lost when an informer—probably Bustos—tipped off the army and on August 30 Tania and the rearguard were betrayed and mown down while fording a river. Only one, a Bolivian, survived. After seeing the guerrillas' bodies on a newsreel, Che's support team back in Cuba watched a Ronald Reagan movie, such was their indifference to their comrade's fate. When Che heard of Tania's death a week later, he refused to believe it. Che's group of between twenty and twenty-five guerrillas were now being pursued by two divisions of the Bolivian army, along with a battalion of Bolivian Rangers—more than 1,500 men in all.

On September 26, Che entered the village of La Higuera, where he pulled some teeth and made a speech. He noted that there were only women in the village. The men had fled to inform the authorities. They reported that 'Guevara appeared sick and exhausted; he rode a mule and appeared unable to walk without support.'

As the vanguard headed north, they were shot at from a ridge overlooking the road. Three guerrillas were killed, two wounded. Two other Bolivians deserted. One of them was captured four days later and revealed Che's plans. Crazily, he planned to attack and occupy the town of Vallegrande, which the Bolivian army were using as their headquarters. Che, it seemed, wanted one last and glorious fight.

On October 7, they were headed down a ravine when they were spotted by an old woman, who had one crippled and one dwarf daughter. He gave them fifty pesos and told them not to reveal their presence to the army—without much hope that they would remain silent. That night, a band of bearded, emaciated guerrillas were spotted by a potato farmer, who dispatched his son to fetch the army. When the news reached Captain Gary Prado Salmón a few miles away, he set up an ambush.

Che had already split his men up into small squads to explore the narrow creeks ahead to discover if there was any way out of the ravine. At dawn, one group spotted a large body of soldiers on the hills above them. Fearing that the entrance to the ravine might already be blocked, Che ordered his men to lie low in the faint hope that they might not have been spotted. But at 1.30 pm on October 8, the men nearest the mouth of the ravine came under attack. A helicopter and jets flew over, but did not strafe or bomb them. Che then pulled those still able to fight back behind the wounded.

When they came under fire again, a bullet hit Che's M-1 in the barrel and it jammed. The magazine from his pistol had been lost. A second bullet hit his beret; a third wounded him in the leg. Simón 'Willy' Cuba, a Bolivian guerrilla, helped him get away, but their retreat was cut off by a cliff. Three soldiers caught up with them and ordered them to drop their weapons and raise their hands. According to one of the soldiers, Che replied: 'Don't shoot, I am Che Guevara and I am worth more to you alive than dead.'

The Bolivian government later claimed that he had said: 'I am Che Guevara and I have failed.'

In a third version, a Cuban threw down his rifle and said: 'Shit, this is Commander Guevara and he deserves respect.'

Captain Prado was immediately informed of Che's capture. Though the firefight was still underway, he scrambled down the ravine and checked his identify. Then he radioed the news to his divisional headquarters in Vallegrande. Che was then marched the mile-and-a-half back to La Higuera. Behind him came a procession of other prisoners and mules carrying the dead and wounded. As they neared the village, hundreds of onlookers lined the route.

Che was thrown into a mud-floored room in the village schoolhouse, bound hand and foot, with the bodies of two dead guerrillas. Willy was locked in an adjoining room. While the Bolivian soldiers celebrated their victory, the authorities deliberated what to do with their celebrity captive. The decision was made early on that Che must die as soon as possible. It seems that the US was not consulted as they had been opposed to the summary execution of Régis Debray. Indeed, Langley sent instructions that the company's men on the spot should 'use all means to keep him alive and have him taken to Panama'.

Captain Prado made some fruitless attempts to interrogate Guevara during the night. However he did talk to Lieutenant Colonel Andrés Selich who asked Che why he seemed so depressed.

'I have failed,' replied Che. 'It's all over, and that's why you see me in such a state.'

Selich also asked Che why he did not fight in his own country and why he and the Cubans had invaded Bolivia. Che insisted that Socialism was the best form of government for Latin America and pointed to his two dead comrades, saying that although they had everything they could want in Cuba they had come to Bolivia to die like dogs. Che then claimed that he was a citizen of Latin America, not just Argentina. He was fighting for the Bolivian peasants, who lived like savages in abject poverty. Selich said that peasants in Cuba suffered the same conditions.

The following dawn his divisional commander Colonel Joaquín Zenteno Anaya and Cuban-American CIA man Felix Rodríguez arrived by helicopter to interrogate the prisoner and photograph his papers. Rodríguez observed that he was in a terrible state. His leg wound oozed blood. His hair was matted. His clothes were matted and torn. And his feet were wrapped in crude sheaths of leather, caked with mud. Che refused to be interrogated, but agreed to enter in an exchange of views. He soon realized that Rodríguez was not Bolivian and, when Rodríguez admitted that he was a Cuban and a member of the CIA-trained anti-Castro 2506 Brigade, Che simply said ha.

But by mid-morning the instructions came through to execute him. When Che heard the news, he blanched. Those present say that he was not ready to die but, after he heard Willy and his other captured comrades being shot, he faced death with dignity and courage. The soldiers drew lots. The task fell to Sergeant Mario Terán, who was instructed not to shoot him in the face. Although several of his comrades in arms had been killed in the ravine, he needed a few swigs of scotch to do the job. According to the official report, Che's last words were: 'I knew you were going to shoot me. I should never have been taken alive. Tell Fidel that this failure does not mean the end of the revolution, that it will triumph elsewhere. Tell Aleida to forget this, remarry and be happy, and keep the children studying. Ask the soldiers to aim well.'

Then, when Terán entered the room, Che is supposed to have said: 'I know you've come to kill me. Shoot, coward, you are only going to kill a man.'

Terán proved he was not a coward with a spray of bullets that ripped though Guevara's body. It was not a painless death, but it was mercifully quick.

Guevara's body was lashed to the skid of the helicopter and flown to Vallegrande, where it was put on display in the laundry room of the hospital of Our Lady of Malta. He was deliberately washed and tidied up, and his beatific expression in the press photos that were taken make him look Christ-like. This image had an enormous impact around the world. The next day his body disappeared. The head of the army General Alfredo Ovando ordered the head and hands to be amputated and the rest of the body cremated, so that no shrine could be built. The CIA were against the decapitation though. Only the hands were removed. They were preserved in formaldehyde and found their way back to Cuba, thanks to a dissident Bolivian minister.

On the night of October 8, while Che lay trussed on the school-house floor, Aleida awoke three thousand miles away in Cuba with a terrible premonition. The following afternoon Fidel's aides arrived with news that Che had been captured, then that he was dead of his wounds. Soon pictures came down the wires and it was confirmed that the corpse belonged to Che.

Castro went on television on October 15 to confirm that Che was dead and declare October 8—the day of Che's last engagement—'The Day of the Heroic Guerrilla'. On October 18 he addressed a crowd of nearly a million, saying: 'If we want the... model of a human being who does not belong to our time but to the future, I say from the depths of my heart that such a model, without a single stain on his conduct, is Che. If we wish to express what we want our children to be, we must say from our very hearts as ardent revolutionaries: we want them to be like Che.'

This caused a profound rift with the Soviet Union where articles were published condemning Che's 'adventurism.' Other Latin American guerrillas inspired by Che rose up. All failed to some degree; most died. Castro tried to go it alone economically, but failed. He had no alternative but to turn back to his patrons in Moscow and Che disappeared from view for fifteen years, though his African policy continued with Cuban troops fighting on in Angola until 1989. While Che Guevara remained a revolutionary icon on campuses in the West, little was heard of him in Cuba until 1991. The figure of Che only resurfaced when Castro turned against Mikhail Gorbachev's liberal policies of *perestroika* and *glasnost*. With the collapse of the Soviet

Union, Cuba had to turn to western tourism to bolster its economy, leaving Che's policies an irrelevance. However the image remained.

In 1967, the Italian publisher Giangiacomo Feltrinelli had stopped off in Havana on his way from Bolivia to Milan to pick up some pictures of Che. He selected Korda's 1960 funeral picture, showing Che with his black beret with the red star on it, staring into the distance. When Che died, Feltrinelli used the photograph to make a poster which was picked up by Italian students who were mourning his death. As Castro did not recognize the 1886 Berne Convention for the Protection of Artistic Works there was no copyright to pay. And in the student protests of 1968 the image appeared across the world. Since then it has appeared on the bedroom walls succeeding generations of students and was prominent at the anti-globalization protest in Cancún in 2003 and the recent "occupy" movements.

Cuba used Guevara's image to attract tourists, whose foreign currency kept the Cuban economy afloat, while Castro's increasingly repressive regime used it to hide behind.

In July 1997, an Argentine-Cuban forensic team discovered the handless skeleton of a man at the bottom of a pit near Vallegrande's dirt airstrip, along with the remains of six other guerrillas. They were exhumed and flown back to Cuba, where they were received at the airport by Aleida and Fidel and Raúl Castro. This was a PR coup for the failing regime In October 1997, Che's body was placed in a reliquary built on the outskirts of Santa Clara, where the last battle of the Cuban Revolution was won, and his canonization was complete.

In 2000, Korda sued the company Smirnoff over the use of his photograph of Che—also known as *Guerillero Heroico* or the Heroic Guerilla—in an advertisement.

'As a supporter of the ideals for which Che Guevara died,' he said, 'I am not averse to its reproduction by those who wish to propagate his memory and the cause of social justice throughout the world, but I am categorically against the exploitation of Che's image for the promotion of products such as alcohol, or for any purpose that denigrates the reputation of Che.'

He donated his out-of-court settlement of $50,000 to the Cuban healthcare system.

'If Che were still alive, he would have done the same,' he said.

He also told a BBC World Service that he approved of the Christ-like 1999 "Che Jesus" adaptation of the image used to promote church attendance in Britain. One can only wonder what Che would have thought of that.

While the image of Che Guevara, the authentic revolutionary went from strength to strength, many of the people involved in the death of Che died in mysterious ways. They were struck down, it was said, by the 'Curse of Che.' The president of Bolivia at the time died in an unexplained helicopter accident in 1969. His successor, one of the cabinet who voted for the execution of Che, was ousted and killed in Argentina. The peasant who betrayed his rearguard was shot. The colonel who identified him from his fingerprints was murdered in Germany. General Zenteno was assassinated in Paris by the mysterious 'Che Guevara International Brigade.' Captain Gary Prado was shot and paralyzed from the waist down. Lieutenant Colonel Selich was beaten to death after rebelling against the Bolivian government. Che's executioner Sergeant Terán lived on in fear of assassination, often adopting a disguise. Rodríguez's career was ended in the 1980s by the Iran-contra hearings.

It seems Guevara had mystical powers even after his death.

Chronology

Year	Age	Life
1928		Born in Rosario, Santa Fé province, Argentina on 14 May or 14 June
1929	1	Leaves father's planation in Misiones to return with family to Buenos Aires
1930	2	First asthma attack
1933	5	The family moves to Alta Gracia in Córdoba
1936	8	Guevara belatedly attends school
1942	14	Begins secondary school in Córdoba
1943	15	Family moves to Córdoba
1948	20	Guevara enters the University of Buenos Aires to study medicine; excused military service because of his asthma
1950	22	Makes 2,500 mile trip on motorised bicycle to northern Argentina
1951	23	Travels from Buenos Aires to Venezuela with Albert Granado
1952	24	Returns to Buenos Aires via Miami to complete studies
1953	25	Qualifies as a doctor; takes second trip through Latin America, involving himself in revolution in Bolvia
1954	26	Sees radical government headed by Jacobo Arbenz in Guatemala overthrown in US-backed coup; escapes to Mexico where he meets Fidel Castro who is planning his

invasion of Cuba; marries

1956	28	Lands with Castro on Cuba; abandons being the group's doctor and takes up arms as guerrilla leader
1959	31	Following Castro's victory, becomes governor of the National Bank in the new government; marries again
1961	33	Becomes Minister for Industry; speaks out against President Kennedy's policy in Latin America
1961-5	33-7	Travels the world as Cuba's roving ambassador
1965	37	Goes to Africa to fight in the Congo
1966	38	Returns to Latin America to organize guerrilla groups to spark '20 new Vietnams'; travels in disguise to Bolivia
1967	39	Following skirmishes with Bolivian Army, is wounded, captured on 8 October and killed soon after

Further Reading

Anderson, Jon Lee, *Che Guevara – A Revolutionary Life* (Bantam Press, London, 1997) – *a huge tome written largely from Anderson's field research and interviews with people who knew Guevara during his lifetime.*

Castañeda, Jorge G., *Compañero – The Life and Death of Che Guevara* (1987; trans Jeremy Leggart; Bloomsbury, London, 1997) – *an accessible book compiled largely from published material, supplement with a large number of interviews.*

Castro, Fidel, *Che – A Memoir* (Ocean Press, Melbourne, 1994) – *a unique insight into Che as a revolutionary and thinker by the man who shaped his life, compiled from speeches, interviews and essays.*

Gadea, Hilda, *Ernesto – A Memoir of Che Guevara*, (trans: Carmen Molina and Walter I. Bradbury, WH Allen, London, 1973) – *entitled* Che Guevara – Años decusivos (*Aguilar, Mexico City, 1972*) *in Spanish, his first wife recounts the story of her life with Che during the crucial years of their meeting in Guatemala in 1954 to their divorce in 1959. It also contains accounts by other people who knew him.*

Gález, William, *Che in Africa* (trans Mary Todd; Ocean Press, Melbourne, 1999) – *the story of Che's year in Africa, incorporating Guevara's lost Congo Diaries.*

Guerava, Ernesto 'Che', *Bolivian Diary* (trans Carlos P Hansen and Andrew Sinclair; Pimlico, London, 2000) – *the most widely read of Che's books which tells the tale of this tragic end.*

Guerava, Ernesto 'Che', *The African Dream – The Diaries of the Revolutionary War in the Congo* (trans Patrick Camiller; Harvill Press, London, 2000) – *Che's own record of his catastrophic adventure in Africa and the first failure of his ideological dream, which would eventually perish the jungles of Bolivia.*

Guerava, Ernesto 'Che', *Guerilla Warfare* (Penguin Books, Harmondsworth, 1961) – *the principles of guerrilla warfare deduced by Che from his experiences in the Cuban Revolution. Second only to Mao Tse-tung's* On Guerrilla Warfare, *it became a handbook for peasant revolt in the Third World and essential reading for all armchair revolutionaries.*

Guevara, Ernesto 'Che', *A Journey to Central America* (trans: Patrick Camiller; Harvill Press, London, 2001) – *an autobiographical account of Guevara's second trip through Latin America in the early 1950s, showing his political development along the way from Buenos Aires to Mexico.*

Guevara, Ernesto 'Che', *The Motorcycle Diaries – A Journey around South America* (trans: Ann Wright; Verso, London, 1994) – *a vivid autobiographical account of Guevara's first voyage of discovery – and self-discovery – on a journey from Buenos Aires to Venezula, with a brief sojourn in Miami on the way home.*

Guevara, Ernest 'Che', *Reminiscences of the Cuban Revolutionary War* (trans: Victoria Ortiz; Penguin Books, Harmondsworth) –

Guevara's own account of the war, though later books say that the text was heavily censored by the government in Havana and complain of Ortiz's poor translation.

Guevara Lynch, Ernesto Rafael, *...Aquí un soldado de América* (Sudamericana-Planeta, Buenos Aires, 1987) – *Che's letters to his family from 1953 to 1956.*

Guevara Lynch, Ernesto Rafael, *Mi Hijo el Che* (Editorial Planeta, Barcelona, 1981) – *a father's portrait of his illustrious son, written after his death.*

Franqui, Carlos, *Diary of the Cuban Revolution* (Viking, New York, 1980) – *a day-by-day account of the Cuban revolution including all the communiqués and correspondence, compiled by one of the participants, an early* fidelísta *who later fled the Socialist paradise.*

James, Daniel, *Ché Guevara – A Biography* (Stein and Day, New York, 1969) – *a comprehensive biography written when Guevara was barely cold in the ground compiled largely from press cuttings.*

Korol, Claudia, *El Che y los argentos* (Ediciones Dialectica, Buenos Aires, 1988) – *Che's call to arms to his fellow countrymen from beyond the grave.*

Lavertsky, I., *Ernest Che Guevara* (Progress Publishers, Moscow, 1976) – *a Communist perspective on the life of the party's favourite son.*

Oltuski Enrique, *Vida Calendestina – My Life in the Cuban Revolution* (Wiley, New York, 2002) – *an account of the struggle in the Sierra and serving in government with Che by a comrade in arms but an ideological enemy.*

Rojo, Ricardo, *Mi Amigo el Che* (trans: Thomas and Carol Christensen; Editorial Jorge Alvarez, Buenos Aires, 1968) – *the unreliable memoir of a friend, rushed out after Che's death. There is also a French version*: Che Guevara – Vie et Mort d'un Ami (*trans*: *Marie-France Rivière*; *Éditions du Seuil, Paris, 1968*).

If you enjoyed *Che Guevara: The Last Conquistador* you might be interested in *The Empress of South America* by Nigel Cawthorne, also published as an ebook by Endeavour Press.

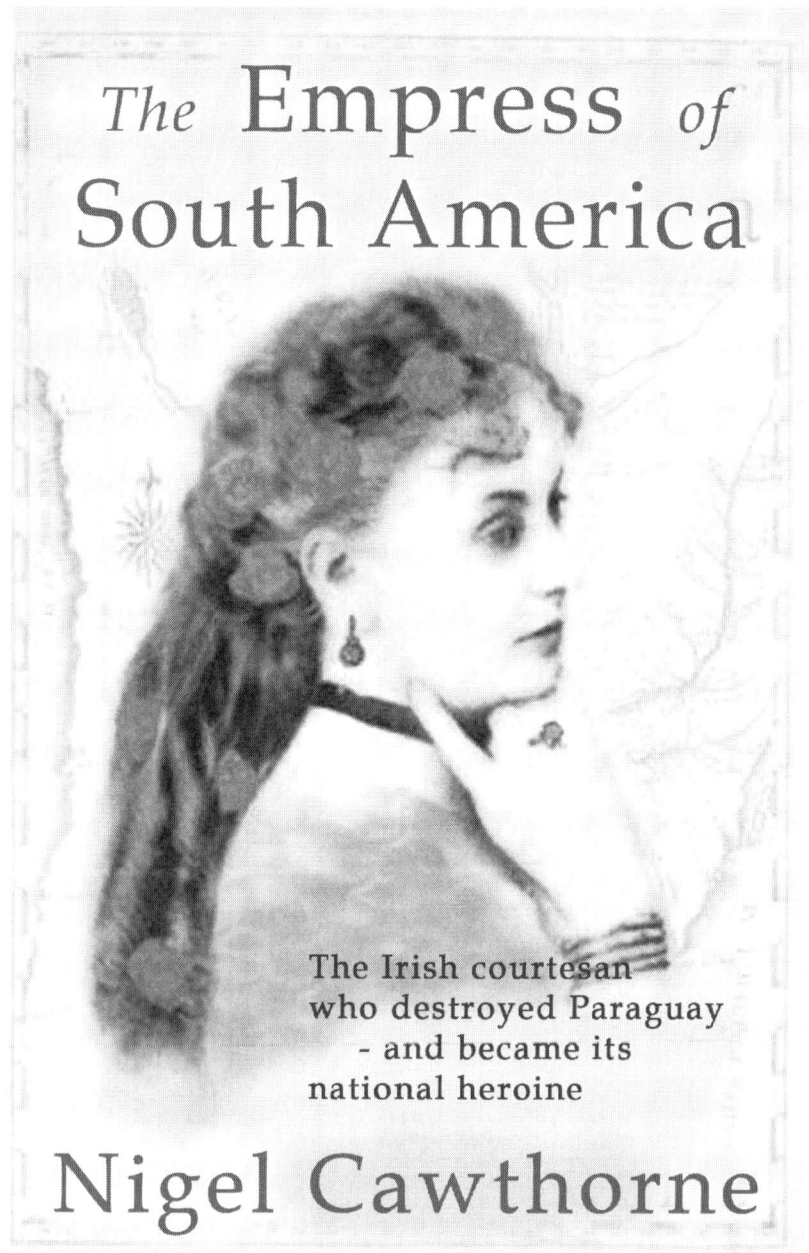

The *Empress of*
South America

The Irish courtesan
who destroyed Paraguay
- and became its
national heroine

Nigel Cawthorne

Extract from *The Empress of South America* by **Nigel Cawthorne**

1 – A National Heroine

One night in May 1961, a Paraguayan of Lebanese descent named Teófilo Chammas scaled the walls of Père Lachaise cemetery in Paris. The gates were locked but the high walls were not topped with barbed wire as they are today. Nor was the cemetery patrolled at night. Then, as now, young lovers climbed into the graveyard to lose themselves in the darkness there.

Chammas, however, had something altogether more dubious in mind. Once inside, Père Lachaise made his way down the Avenue Carette, past the tomb of Oscar Wilde, to Division 92 of the cemetery. There he began searching for plot number 6/42 –18/90. The nearest landmark was the reclining brass figure of journalist Victor, Noir whose lips and crotch have been burnished by the countless caresses of female mourners lavished on his effigy since he was shot by Prince Pierre Bonaparte in 1870, hastening the end of the Second Empire. Six rows behind Noir and eighteen from the Avenue Carette, Chammas found what he was looking for.

At the foot of the ornamental sarcophagus at plot 6/42 – 18/90 was the label 'C. *A*.P.' – Concession à Perpétuité – ' *No* 542 *année* 1886'. An inscription on the lid of the sarcophagus noted that the tomb belonged to the *Famille Martin*. The grave, according to another inscription, housed

221

one Estelle Martin, who had died on February18th, 1900. But it was not Estelle Martin that Chammas was interested in. There were other curious clues on the sarcophagus. On one side there was the puzzling legend *Paz y Justicia* – 'peace and justice' in Spanish. Beneath it was the figure of a dancing lion holding, on a stick, a Phrygian cap – once worn by freed Roman slaves, but better known as the French Revolutionary's 'red cap of liberty'. This figure was borrowed from the great seal of Paraguay. The other side of the sarcophagus bore the five-pointed star and olive branch of the Paraguayan flag. At the end of the sarcophagus nearest Victor Noir there was an escutcheon bearing three stylised shamrocks. Above it appeared a wolf; below, the motto read: *Lupus me fugit inermen* – 'The wolf flees from me though I am unarmed'.

Although the meaning of these inscriptions would have been lost on the casual visitor, they would have told Chammas that he was in the right place. To those familiar with the troubled past of South America, their significance would have been explained by a small marble plaque on the other end of the sarcophagus, which said in Spanish:

Monument erected

by

Enrique, Federico and Carlos Solano López.

To the illustrious memory

of their always beloved and unforgettable mother

Doña Elisa Alicia Lynch-López.

Died 25 July 1886.

Reading this, students of Latin American history would instantly recall the bloodiest war in the history of the Americas, a war which left more dead that the United States' bitter Civil War and all but destroyed a wealthy nation, through the weakness of a man and the ambition of a woman. It was this woman, Elisa Alicia Lynch– López – better known as Eliza Lynch – that Chammas had come for.

A freelance import–exporter and general entrepreneur, Chammas was new to the grave–robbing business, but he had cultivated useful contacts among the staff at Père Lachaise. Money had changed hands and the tomb had already been opened. There were five coffins in the grave. The first two occupants were Estelle Martin and Eliza Lynch. They had been buried there in May, 1900. Estelle Martin had died in February of that year and had been interred briefly elsewhere, while Eliza had languished in a tiny grave in Division 53 of Père Lachaise since July 27th, 1886. As these two had been buried first, the other coffins were stacked up on top of them, making exhumation difficult. Manhandling a coffin out of a grave is a strenuous and time-consuming business at the best of times and coffins that had lain in the damp soil of Père Lachaise for any length of time would have been in a fragile state. So by the time Chammas reached those of Estelle and Eliza, it must have been nearing dawn.

According to Chammas, when he finally opened what he took to be Eliza's coffin, the corpse's long, black hair turned instantly to luminous gold. This may have just been hyperbole, but perhaps, at very moment he opened the coffin, the first rays of the spring sun burst over the horizon, bathing the corpse in golden spring sunlight. He certainly would not have been able to linger over the scene. Daylight would bring the workmen who tended the graves and officials who ran the cemetery. Soon after, Père Lachaise would be open to visitors. Chammas was certainly not eager to be caught. He hurriedly packed up Eliza's remains and made his escape.

At around this time the Paraguayan Ambassador to Paris, Dr Hipólito Sánchez Quell, was making official representations to the French government, formally requesting the return of the remains of Eliza Lynch. Although Eliza was an Irish woman, British by birth, French by marriage and Parisian by inclination, Paraguayan dictator General Alfredo Stroessner believed that her body belonged in Paraguay. The appropriate paperwork was lodged with the French authorities and, while the bureaucracy went slowly about its business, Dr Quell paid a visit to Eliza's grave with his ten-year-old daughter. It would have come as a shock to him when he discovered that Madame Lynch's remains had already been disinterred and had been hurried out of the country. But Dr Quell had no doubt who was responsible – a fellow countryman who he denounced as the chief *contrabandista*.

While Dr Quell had been seeking the removal of the remains through the proper channels, Chammas smuggled the corpse back to South America in a coffin packed with Lebanese hashish. It was intercepted by customs at Buenos Aires. From Argentina, the remains either travelled on to Paraguay in a gunboat after some diplomatic arrangement had been stitched together, or Chammas, a drug smuggler who had turned grave–robber to ingratiate himself to the dictator Stroessner, paid off the Argentine customs officials, chartered a seaplane and look Eliza's remains back to Paraguay in a suitcase.

At least that is one version of the story. Bizarre, certainly. But it would have been a fitting postscript the life of a truly remarkable woman. There are, of course, more prosaic accounts of her return to Paraguay.

The French authorities insist that Eliza Lynch was legally exhumed. The records clerk at Père Lachaise even says that the Paraguayan

Ambassador was there when she was disinterred, though the cemetery records are closed to the general public. However, under French law, it is necessary to have the consent of the next of kin of all the people buried in a grave before it can be disturbed. The Prefecture of Police had the consent of Jorge Manuel and Elisa A. Solano López, Eliza Lynch's grandchildren, to remove her body. But it would have been difficult, if not impossible, to track down the families of the four other people buried there.

The Paraguayan authorities also maintain that the exhumation was carried out legally. But strangely, Dr Quell, who was both a prolific writer and passionate devotee of Madame Lynch, makes no reference to her exhumation in the extensive volumes he wrote about his endeavours in Paris, even though the return of Eliza's remains would surely have been his greatest diplomatic triumph.

The historian at Père Lachaise, Christian Charlet, says that this is easily explained. The request for the return of the remains of Eliza Lynch was handled covertly through the French embassy in Asunción, the capital of Paraguay. The Paraguayan Embassy in Paris was informed later and only discovered that the body was already gone when the ambassador visited Père Lachaise on May 23rd.

'In view of the use made of Elisa Lynch-López's remains when they were returned to Paraguay, it is not impossible that the political power of the time (General– President Alfredo Stroessner) preferred to secure their return via a discreet approach, purely family,' says M. Charlet, 'rather than make an official political intervention that would be likely to provoke a negative reaction from the French Government.'

But the French Government were not that squeamish.

225

President Charles de Gaulle visited Paraguay in 1964, just three years after the remains had been returned. He does not seem to have been bothered by any 'use' the remains were put to. And certainly it would not have been possible for the French President to have visited Paraguay if there was any outstanding dispute between the two countries – over a little grave robbing, say. So perhaps the whole thing was swept under the carpet. After all, it is not very difficult to make the appropriate adjustments to records that are not open to the public.

At the time, the Paraguayans maintained that Madame Lynch's remains were returned on a warship. But landlocked Paraguay did not have any ocean-going warships – and does not to this day. Its naval activity is limited to the three navigable rivers – the Paraguay, the Parana and the Pilcomayo – that mark four-fifths of the borders of modern Paraguay. Nevertheless, the remains did arrive at the dockside in Asunción on 25th July, 1961, the seventy–fifth anniversary of Eliza Lynch's death. General Stroessner, in a uniform befitting the president of a banana republic that grows no bananas, was waiting on the quay. He had proclaimed the day a 'Day of National Homage' and the entire government was present, along with a guard of honour and a huge crowd. As the Paraguayan Army Band struck up Paraguay's operatic national anthem, the remains were brought ashore in a large bronze urn. This urn was identical to one said to contain the remains of another great hero of Paraguayan history, Eliza's lover and partner in crime, Mariscal Francisco Solano López – one-time dictator, former army chief and war hero, who was also variously described as the world's worst tyrant since Nero and the biggest mass murderer since Genghis Khan. Between the two of them they were responsible for the slaughter of practically the entire male population of Paraguay while, behind Francisco's back, Eliza bled the country dry.

However, according to General Stroessner's grandiloquent speech at the quayside, the beautiful Eliza was a national heroine and a national martyr, though she had died far from Paraguay and in much greater comfort than most of her victims. The huge funeral cortege then made its way up the hill to the Panteón de los Heroes – a replica of Napoleon's tomb in Les Invalides – which her consort Francisco had had built to house his own remains. Stroessner's intention was that the two lovers were to be re-united there. He had hoped that the two unlikely national heroes would lie side by side in the Panteón de los Heroes in perpetuity. But, at the last minute, the Catholic Church had raised an objection. Eliza and Francisco had never been married. Throughout her time in Paraguay, Eliza was married to a Frenchman and her liaison with López had been adulterous. The Panteón de los Heroes stood on sanctified ground and, according to the Church, it would be an affront to God for the two of them to lie there together – even though it was unlikely that they would break the seventh commandment again, given the fact that they were dead.

The Church's scruples did not hugely concern Alfredo Stroessner, the strongman who had ruled Paraguay unopposed since he seized power in a coup in 1954 – he would continue to do so until 1989, making him the longest–standing ruler of any South American country in the twentieth century. However, just six years before, he had seen his old friend Juan Peron ousted from Argentina after the Church turned against him. Peron had had the temerity to petition the Pope to have his late wife, the one-time prostitute Eva Perón (née Duarte) – Evita – canonised. And Eliza

Lynch's reputation was no more savoury. Privately Stroessner would accede to the demands of Mother Church. But publicly he was not going to be robbed of his moment of glory. As Pallbearer-in-Chief, Stroessner led Eliza's funeral procession into the Panteón de los Heroes. In a scene rich in symbolism, Eliza's urn was solemnly marched in through the front door of Francisco's mausoleum, then – after the briefest reunion with the supposed remains of her lover – it was whisked out of the back door again.

From there, the remains were spirited down the Avenida Mariscal Francisco Solano López to the Ministry of National Defence. On the second floor, a small 'Museo Madame Lynch' had been prepared in what was essentially a broom cupboard, next to the gentlemen's lavatory. It contained a rusty sword said to have belonged to Francisco López, a book of homage containing some 87,000 signatures and a portrait of the national heroine, showing Eliza's dazzling beauty at its imperious height. There the remains were left to gather dust for the next nine years.

Printed in Great Britain
by Amazon.co.uk, Ltd.,
Marston Gate.